Aernout MIK

primal gestures, minor roles

Stedelijk Van Abbemuseum Eindhoven

NAi Publishers Rotterdam

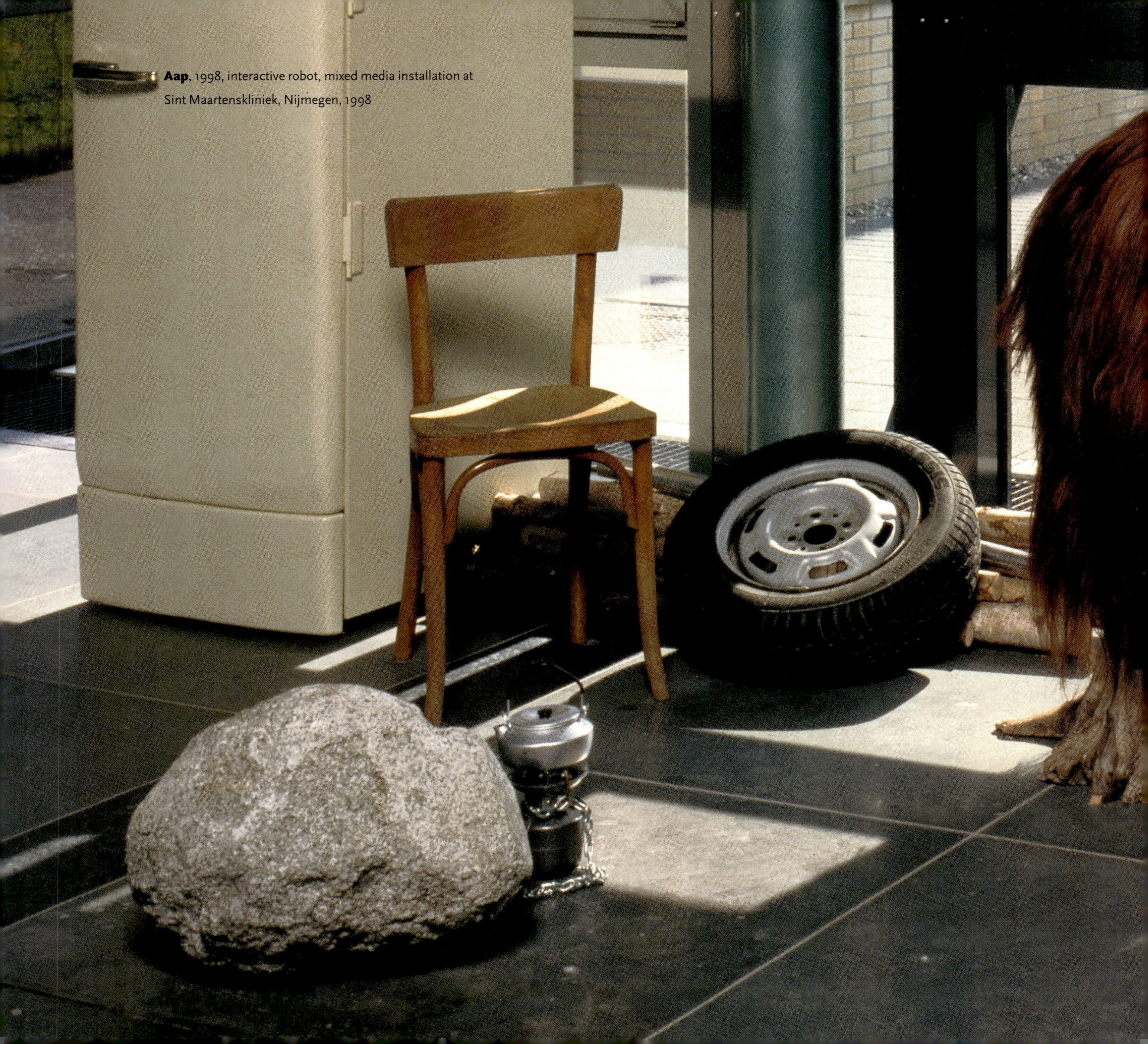

Aap, 1998, interactive robot, mixed media installation at Sint Maartenskliniek, Nijmegen, 1998

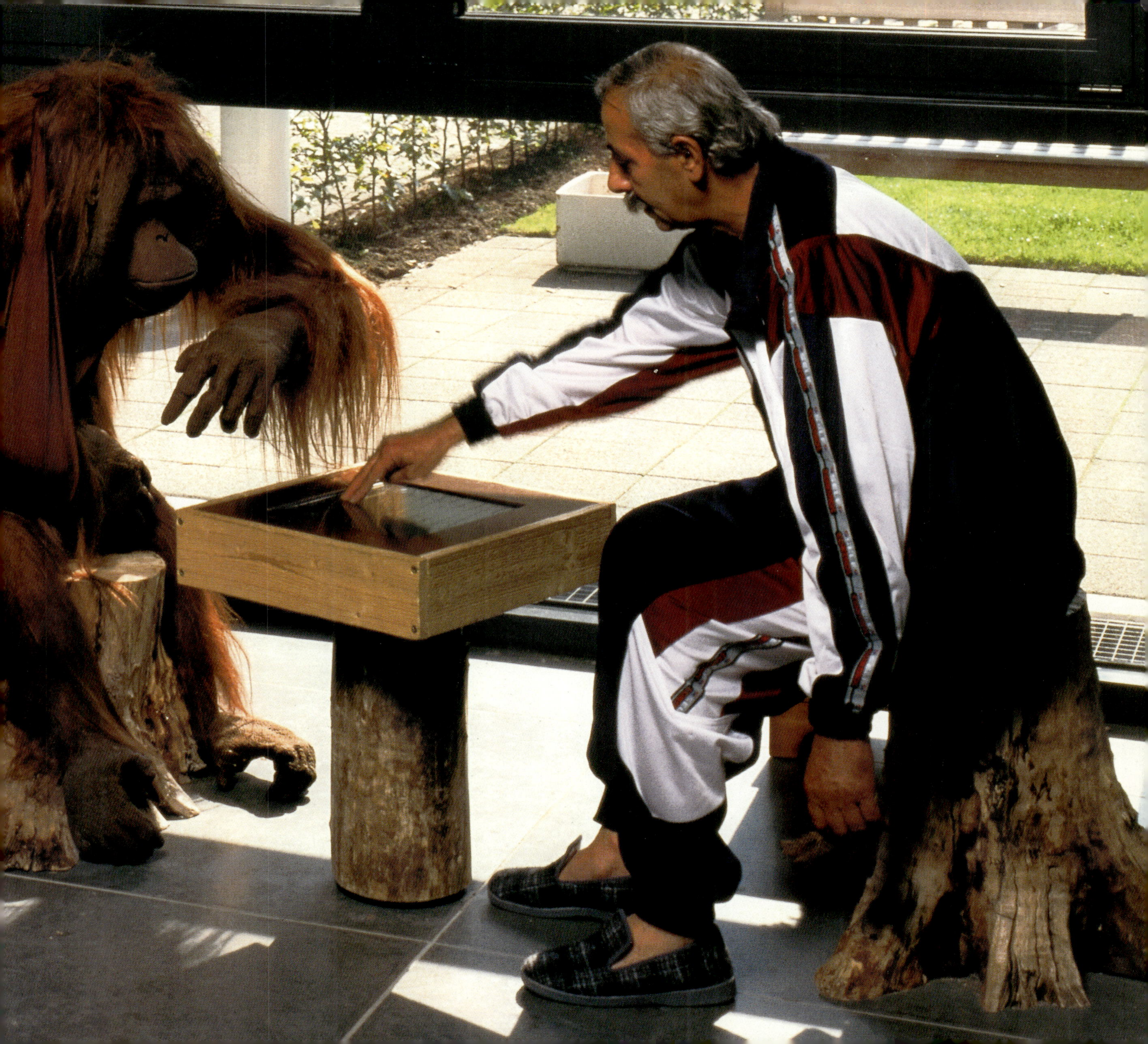

Contents

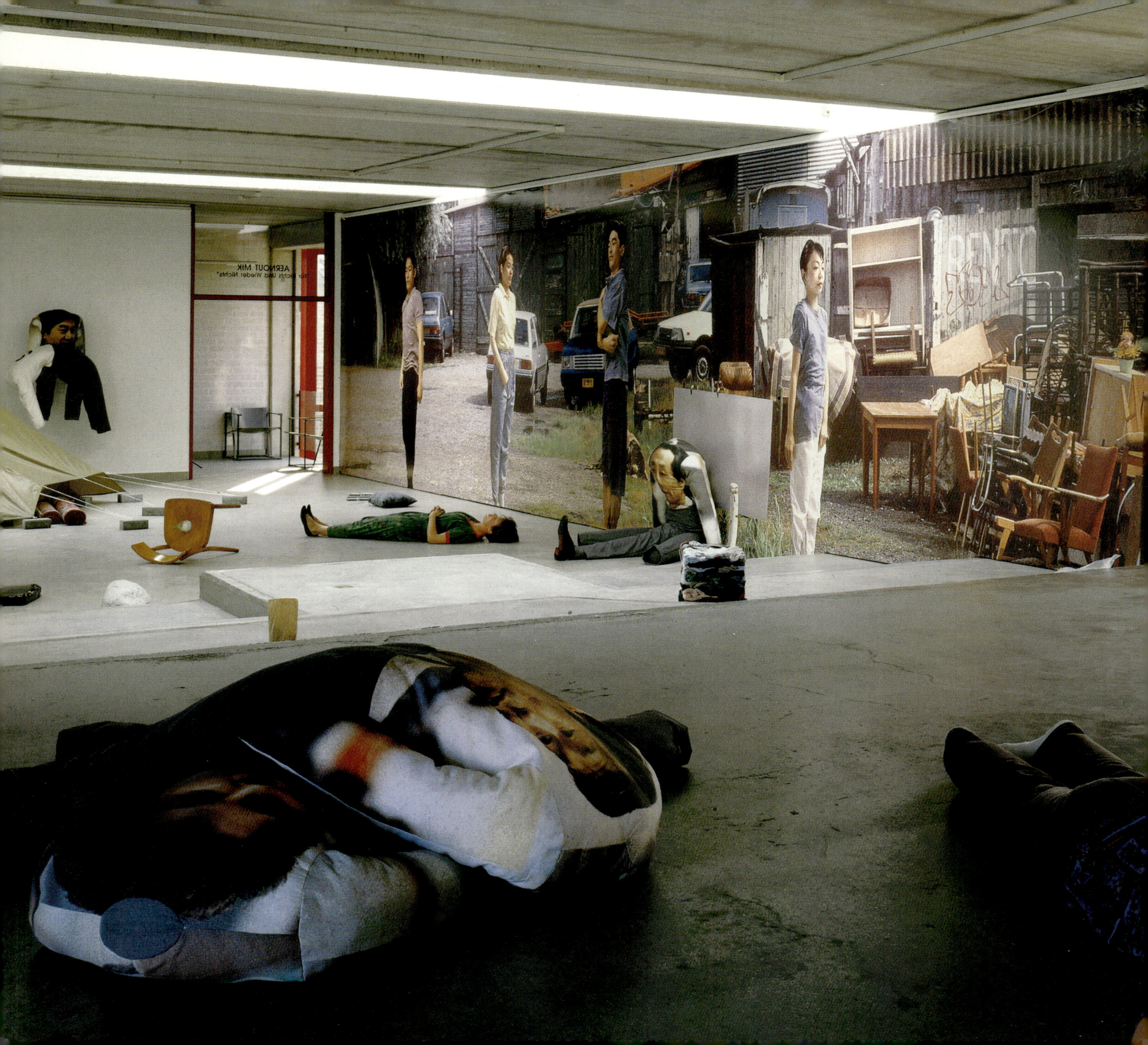
AERNOUT MIK

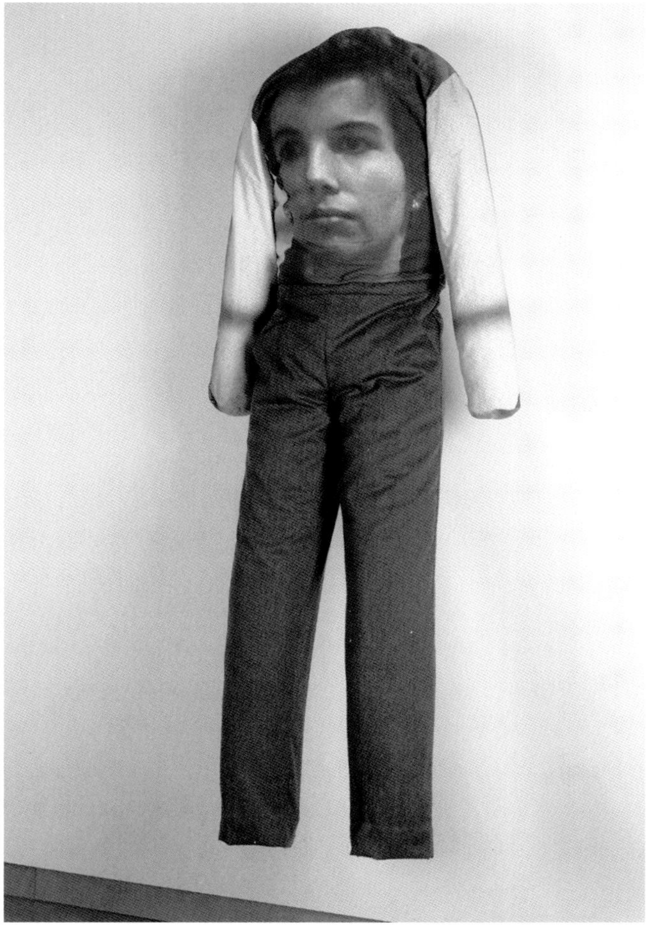

exhibition view Deweer Art Gallery, Otegem (B), 1992, **Für Nichts und Wieder Nichts**, 1992, mixed media installation **Assistant** (from **Für Nichts und Wieder Nichts**), 1992

Miscellaneous Exits for Smaller Animals

A short introduction to the work of Aernout Mik

Jaap Guldemond, Jan Debbaut

In his first solo exhibition in a museum, the Dutch artist Aernout Mik (1962) has completely shaped the Van Abbemuseum to his own will. A circuit of neutral, white rooms has been largely removed to make way for a new, more organic architectural structure. Some elements of the original architecture have been accentuated by Mik, while new elements such as rounded corners, walls not placed at right angles to one another, tapering corridors, heavily reduced wall heights, irregular surfaces and moving parts have been added. Mik has filled this new architecture with videos, objects, photographs and three-dimensional installations. The videos are projected onto transparent screens seamlessly incorporated in the walls. The projections usually reach to the floor, so that a strongly physical, almost sculptural relation is created between the viewer and the projected images. The walls are lower than usual in many places so that you can just see over the top of them, and the objects often differ in size from the original. All these spatial corrections and additions produce a situation in which the visitor actively experiences the whole architecture.

This spatial intervention in the Van Abbemuseum is typical of how Aernout Mik strips standardised situations and spaces of their usual function. He dislocates socially determined patterns (of expectation) of human behaviour. He deploys various resources to change what he calls the 'dynamics of a situation' so that the visitor can experience it physically.
The contradictory relation between the space itself and the human behaviour that Mik introduces into it is interesting in this connection. This is particularly true of his video works. Many of them show spaces in which a number of people are exposed to external manipulations and events without actively reacting to them. The characters are immobile, like objects, while the space is in motion and becomes an almost living organism. Floors move, a sticky substance flies into the space from outside, dust / soil fall out of the air, an enormous quantity of foam slowly takes over the space, and so on. For instance, in the video *Float* (1998) two people lie flat on the ground while the space in which they are situated shakes roughly up and down and makes their bodies jerk like puppets. In *Lick* (1996) two girls are sitting with their backs leaning against a wall, while a blue liquid intermittently spurts from their chest. Sometimes their bodies rise briefly from the floor. Opposite them a man resting on his knees slides vertically up through the screen in a slow, mechanical movement. A tube emits grey mud. All the movements seem to merge into a 'breathing' whole.

A similar role as objects is assigned to the extras Mik sometimes employs for his installations. They sit, sleep, lie down, hang or fool around, thereby acquiring a subdued, sculptural form of presence. They seem to be keener on entering into an alliance with the furniture and objects that surround them than on engaging in active behaviour. In *Wie die Räume gefüllt werden müssen* (1995) Mik set three extras on a mezzanine in the Kunstverein in Hanover. The three girls, dressed in German police uniforms, did nothing except lie down, sit or talk to one another a little. They were present,

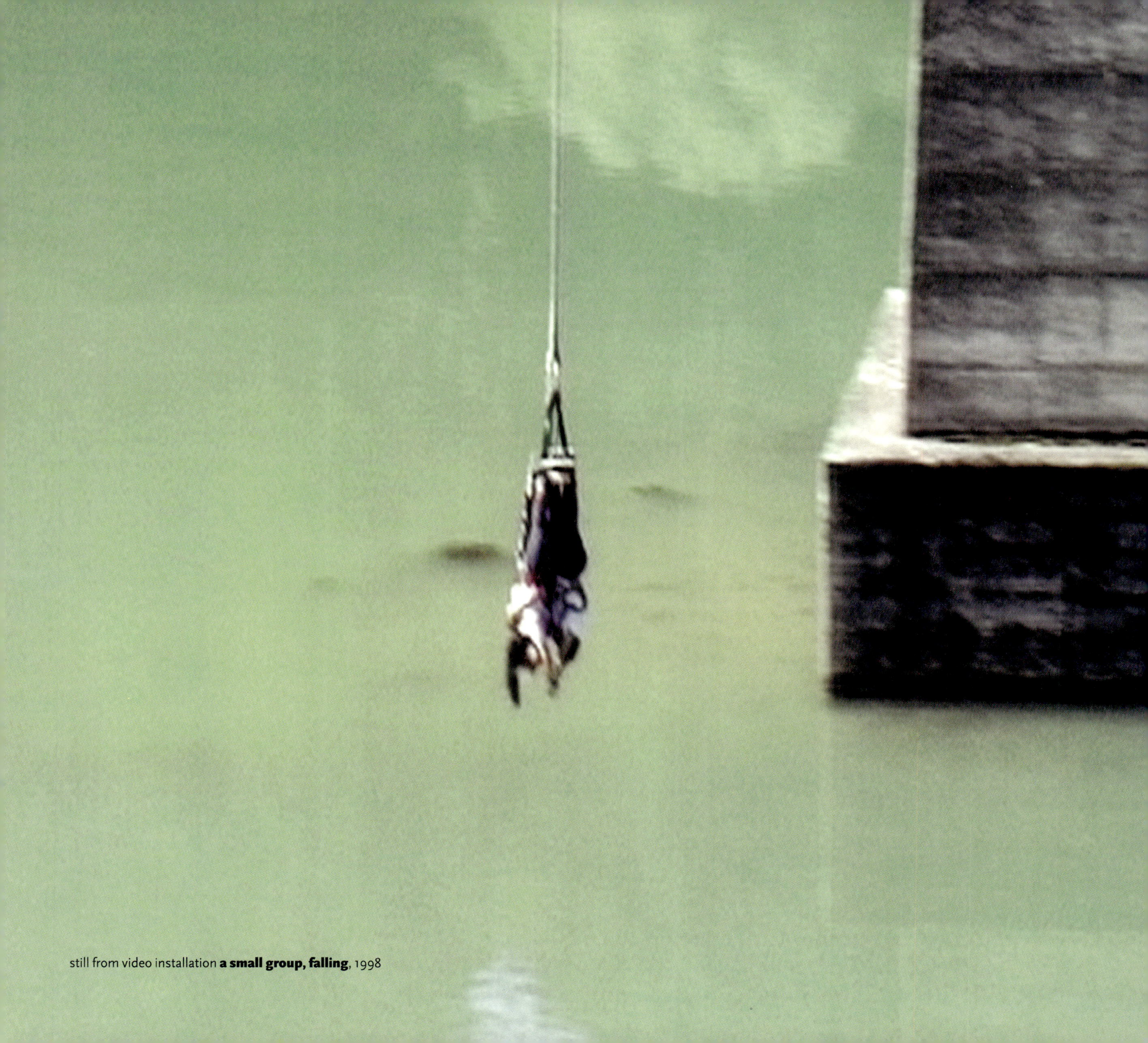

still from video installation **a small group, falling**, 1998

nothing more. Mik had installed the mezzanine in the space so that the scene could only be seen – and with difficulty – from the adjacent rooms. This conveyed the impression that the scene was self-engrossed, outside or next to the different reality of the other rooms.
It is as if different realities have been brought together in the same space in Mik's video installations too. Not only is there a schism in the video images themselves between the persons and their surroundings, but a schism also arises between the reality of the architectural space in which the video screens are incorporated as a logical component, on the one hand, and the world of the protagonists in the videos, on the other. As the projections are at floor level and the people in them are almost life size, they seem to have as much of a reality of their own as the viewers themselves.

As an extension of these two 'methods', Mik applies a third form to set the 'dynamics of a situation' in motion, to change it, or to trigger it. In his live videos Mik combines the presence of extras with the use of video projection. A good example is *Parallel Bar*, a work that Mik recently produced in Ottawa, Canada. An empty shop was converted into a sort of coffee bar, a place to which people could retreat briefly from the bustle of the street. He inserted two large transparent screens in a wall and projected an everyday scene onto them: a number of people sitting on chairs and sofas talking and drinking together. However, now and then they disturb their activities with unexpected behaviour: they walk backwards and forwards through a doorway, bang it shut with a loud crash, open their mouth wide without making a noise, or drill in a table with an electric drill. That this scene is actually taking place at the same moment in the space behind the screens can only be surmised from the fact that the sound of the actual scene without any amplification can be heard directly in the coffee bar. The rift between what are taken to be live projected video images and hearing the actual sound is almost unbridgeable. It seems practically impossible to get the two to merge in a single experience. This disruption is further reinforced because the scene is simultaneously filmed from two different positions. Each of them seems to show a completely different space, but both cameras are focused on the same scene.

Recent videos like *Mob* (1998) and *Piñata* (1999) reveal yet another aspect of Mik's work: a form of human behaviour that is neither passive nor sculptural, but characterised precisely by play, obsession and release. These videos feature groups of people who are engaged in a series of activities without any apparent logic. In *Mob* this produces the sense of watching a sports contest without knowing the rules of the game. *Piñata* is dominated by an element of obsessive release. Two, almost overlapping video screens, show a group of people in an unspecified room. The floor is littered with dozens of flesh-coloured blocks of polystyrene foam. Once again a strange scene unfolds before the viewer's gaze – filmed directly and without sound, as in all of Mik's videos. Ten people, like a group of wild animals, indulge in a subdued orgy of introverted violence. At the same time a brown substance falls now and then from the air and covers the whole scene.

This interchange of human and animal behaviour can be found more often in Mik's universe. Mik's interest in hybrid forms in general, and in those of human and animal behaviour in particular, is expressed in countless installations which feature not only extras, dolls, dummies and animals, but also androids and other mechanically driven figures. Animal, human and mechanical actions constantly merge in a single space. The organic and the non-organic, the genuine and the artificial, become entangled and merge.

No matter how strange the situations Mik presents may be, they are never experienced as a complete opposite to reality. They are situations which jar with reality, and thereby charge the space. Mik achieves this by always embedding his situations in the last resort in the real world we know. Primal gestures, minor roles. They are incomplete, open, heterogeneous constellations that may elude us rationally, but return to us through other senses.

The Van Abbemuseum has followed, exhibited and incorporated several pieces of Aernout Mik's work in its collection since 1991. He participated for instance in a preview of the Dutch submission to the 21st São Paulo Biennale (1991), the international group exhibition 'ID' (1996), and showed the joint project with Marjoleine Boonstra *Hongkongoria* in connection with the exhibition 'NL' (1998).
This presentation is in line with the museum's policy of entering into a longer term commitment with a relatively small group of artists. That is why the Van Abbemuseum is delighted to be able to offer Aernout Mik the opportunity to present a large number of recent and older works for the first time in an entirely new constellation. We hope that this exhibition, and especially this publication, will contribute to a wider understanding of Mik's œuvre, both in the Netherlands and abroad.

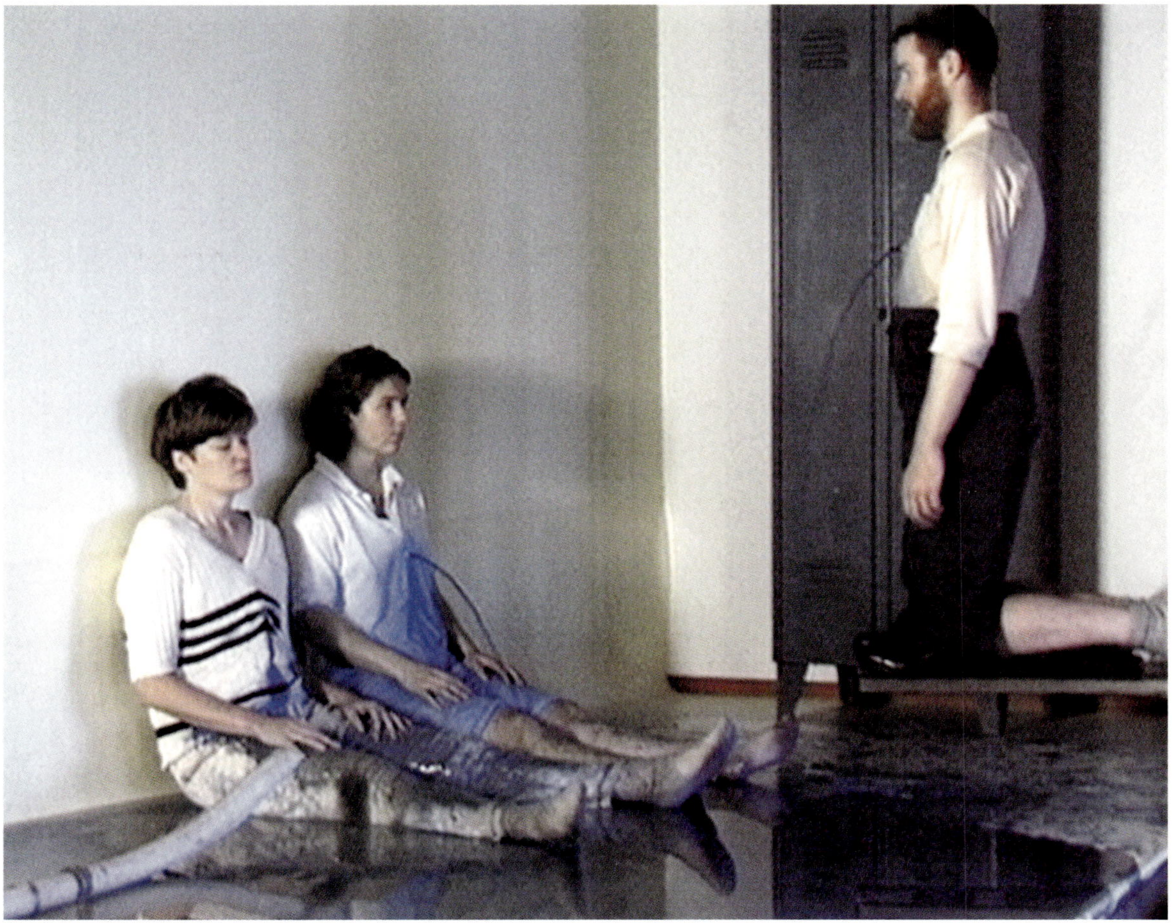

still from video installation **Lick**, 1996

exhibition view 'ID', Stedelijk Van Abbemuseum, Eindhoven, 1996

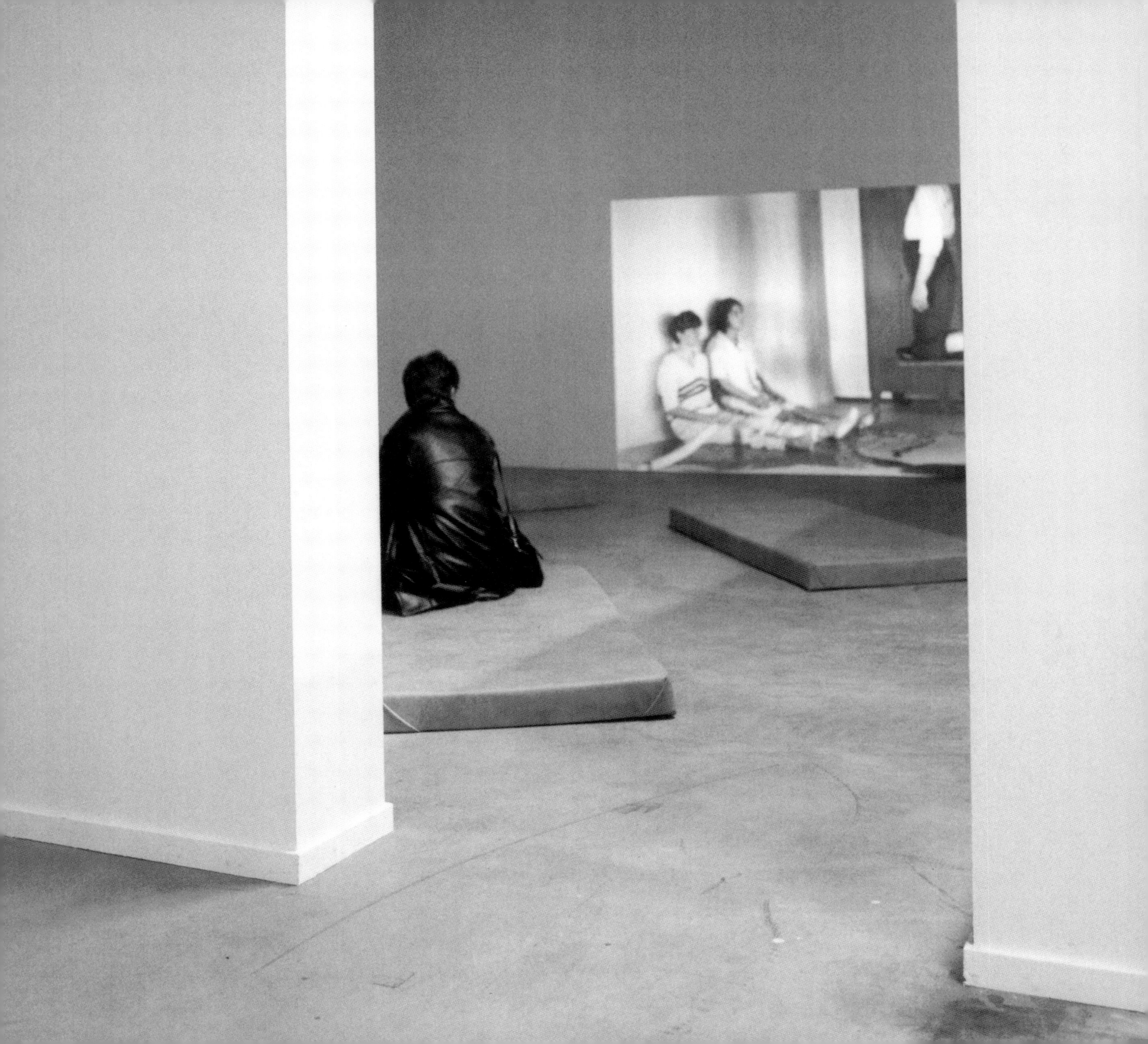

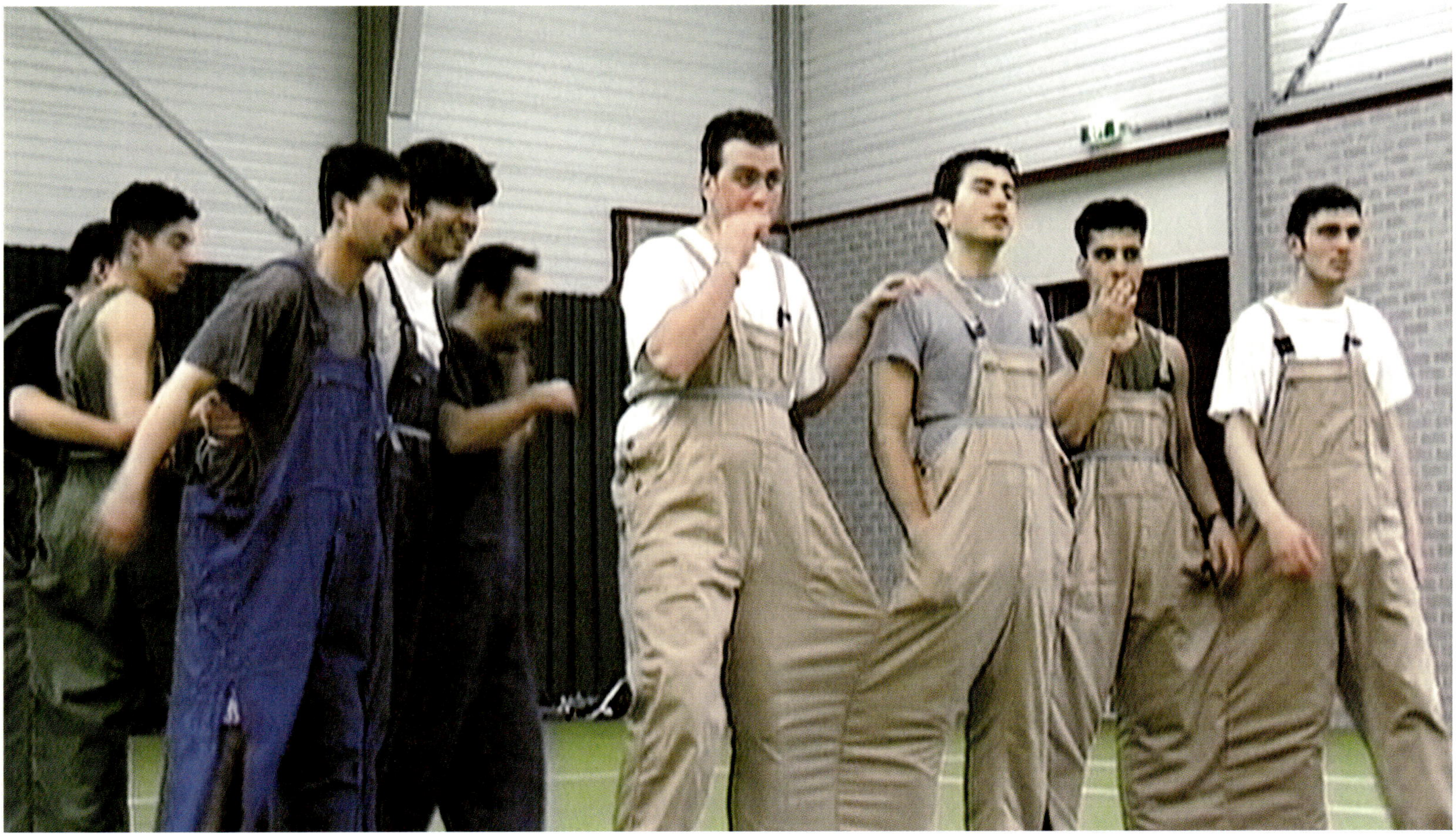

stills from video installation **Mob**, 1998

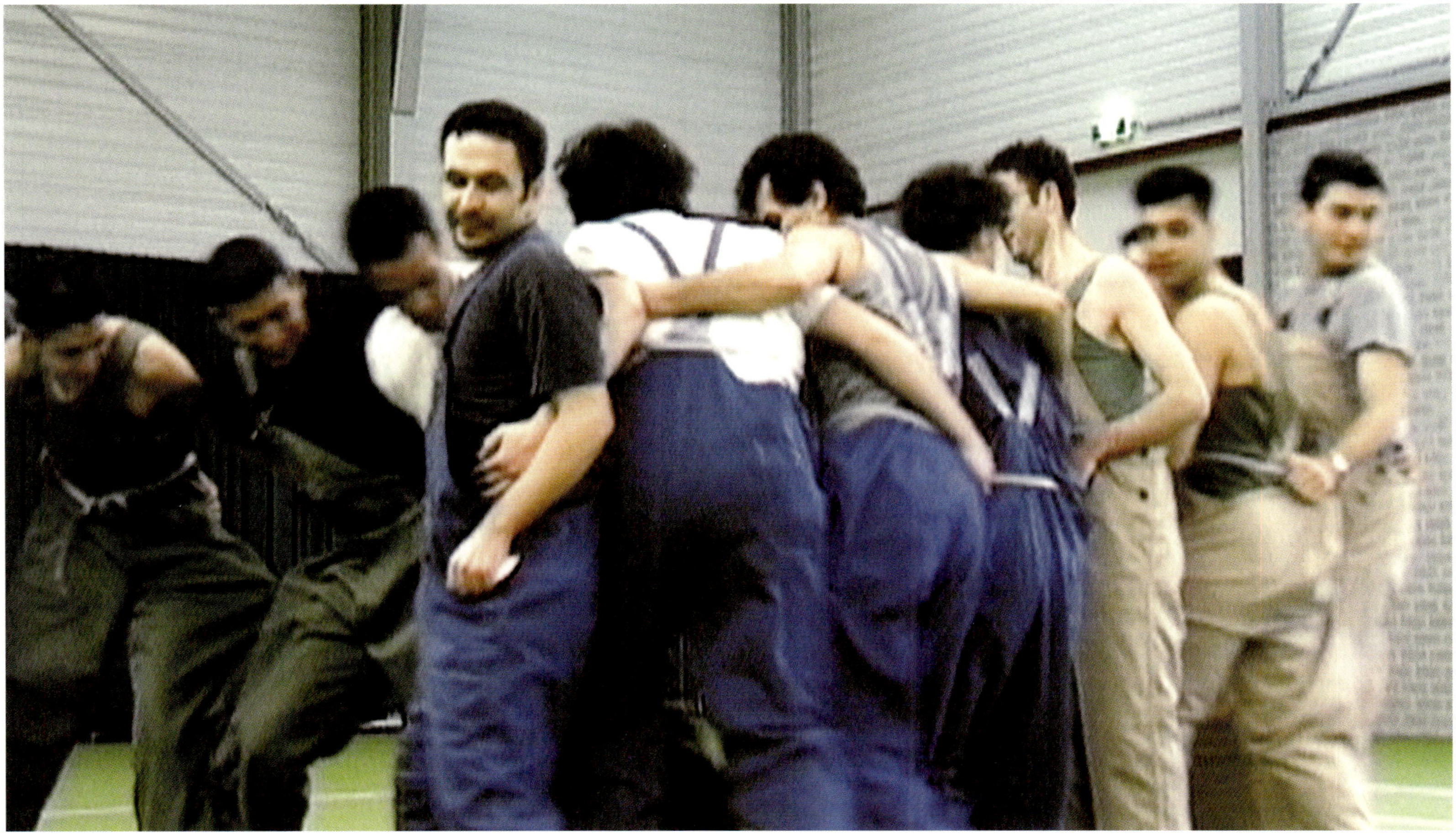

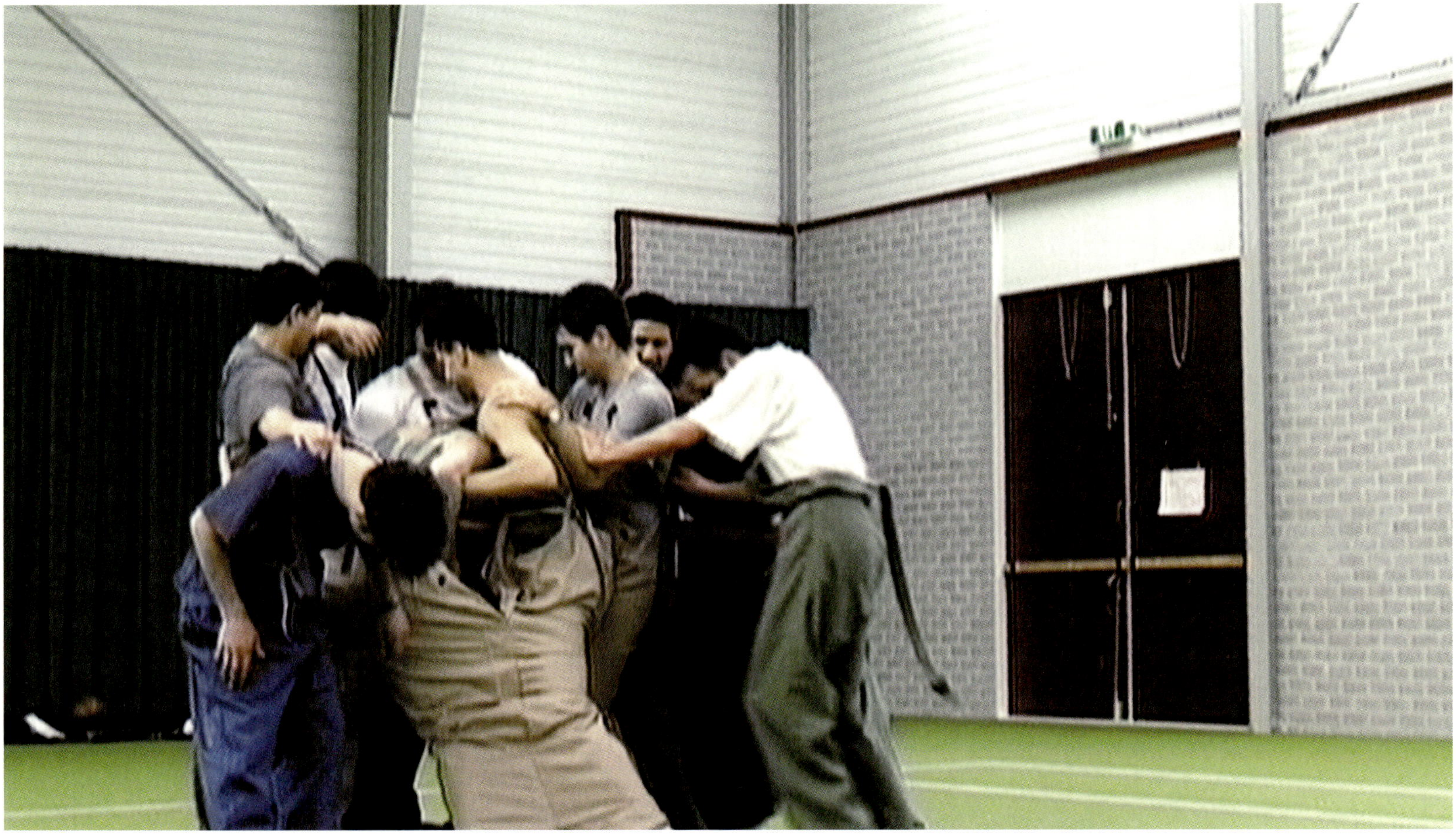

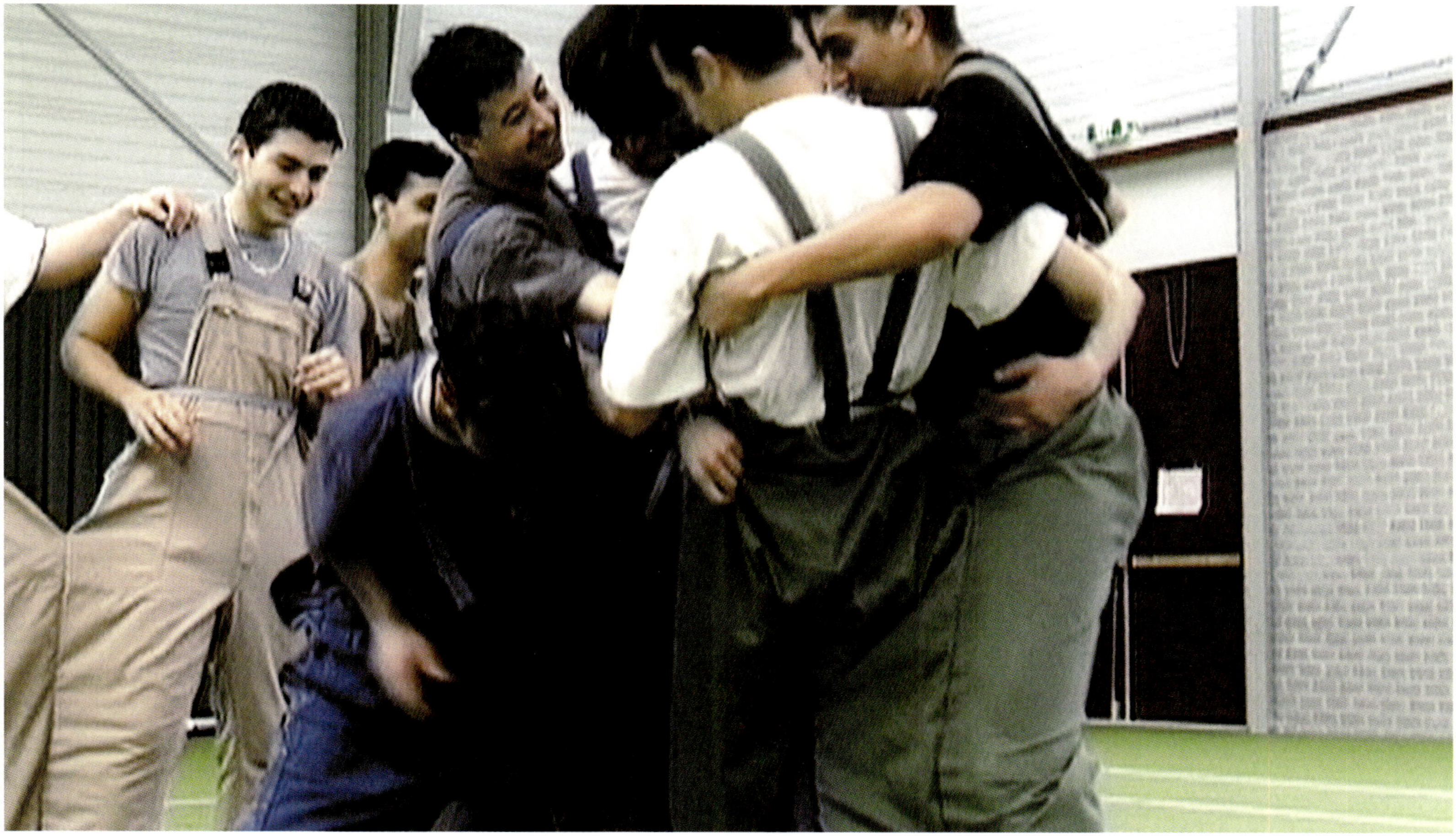

Systemic Gut Twisting

Bernhard Balkenhol

In the introduction to his book *The Negative Horizon*, Paul Virilio describes a strange experiment in perception. Still a painter in those days, he was fascinated with the observation that, as soon as he moved but kept an eye on the objects he had been looking at, an interesting life of continually changing forms began, behind and in front of the objects which we naturally perceive, dominantly and selectively. '... No longer did I have only the choice between "negative" and "positive", those arbitrary terms, but between form and its continuation, antiform.' Virilio trained his eye to suspend the hierarchy of things and the spaces in between them to define given forms by their exteriors. He asked himself: 'Has such a hierarchy always existed? Or was it gradually built up by experience, by the lifestyles of groups and societies past? Would it be possible to continue living by perceiving the world in contrary: by perceiving the nothingness, transparency with figures in the foreground, all matter in the centre and objects as background, no longer as forms? ... My continual efforts to live this way created enormous difficulties for me and demanded an extraordinary amount of will power in every respect.'

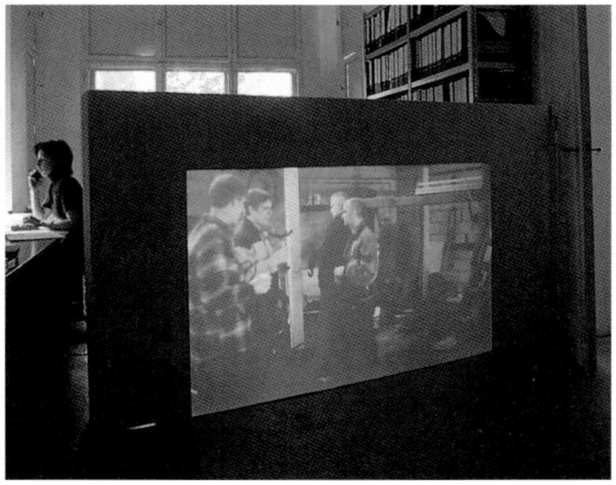

exhibition view 'Softer Catwalk in Collapsing Rooms',
Galerie Gebauer, Berlin, 1999,
Garage, 1998, video installation

A man and a woman are lying relaxed and belly-down on the ground next to a brickwall. They are so relaxed because the ground beneath them is rising and falling rythmically and irregularly so that their bodies are thrown up and down. The two do not seem to be very affected by it, they manifest neither pleasure nor annoyance. They do not defend themselves nor engage themselves in the movement – they simply let go. In Aernout Mik's video *Float* (1988), there is no indication of any other possible behaviour. In addition, as though the artist were mocking the situation, before the wall where the images are projected life-size, a mattress lies for the viewer himself.

What would happen if the hierarchy of forms in space were suspended? If content and significance, cause and effect could float freely?

Regardless of how unusual and strange the scenes in Mik's video installations appear, the viewer soon turns from fascinated observation and examination to speculation about the causes and backgrounds of what he sees. However, the search for purpose eventually defuses, because what we are looking at is an actual place and actual persons, that is, a real fate that the eye at least can comprehend. The installation has the effect of wallpaper: the principle of an endless sequence develops a decorative pattern, and the result is that the pictures' motifs and content disappear. One does not deal with wallpaper, one lives in it and enjoys the ambience created by it.

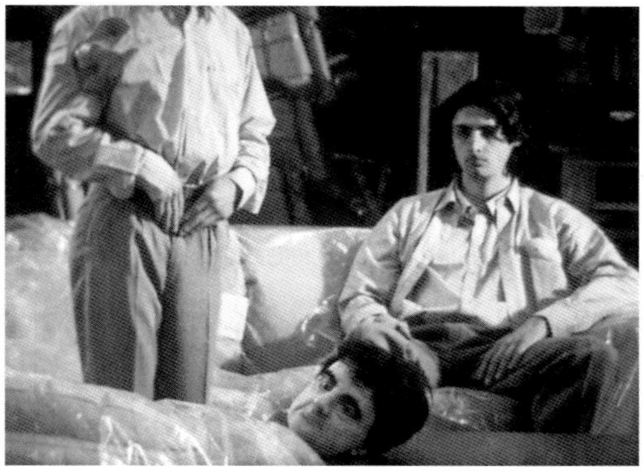

still from video installation **Fluff**, 1996

Reconstruction in one's perception is exhausting as the different layers which constitute the picture must be isolated and looked at individually against one's preconceptions and against the 'wallpaper effect'. The tossed up couple arouses the most diverse associations, from a fun course at a fair to a therapeutic exercise, from rhythmical pairing on a mattress to an earthquake. The search for content and for unambiguous interpretation is continually disturbed by a structure, a moiré of displaced layers which our understanding must surmount.

In a garage, three men stand and walk around, drinking mineral water. Inexplicably, they do not swallow the water but spit it out casually or let it run down from their mouth onto their clothes without paying any notice, like in a film playing in reverse. Five individuals altogether (appearing in alternating combinations), they are unique but typical of a garage. They appear to wait or take breaks, they have nothing to do and nothing happens. Then suddenly, as though from a tacit cue or perhaps in a fit, two of them shove a third one out of the picture. All returns to 'normal' immediately thereafter. This scene repeats itself in various variations without any dramatic changes, endlessly. It was at Berlin's Gebauer Gallery in 1999 where Aernout Mik exhibited this video loop *Garage* (1988) in the gallery's office. It was installed on such a scale that the normal activities and the visitors completed the scene: similar incidents were expected to occur in the gallery just as in the video.

One never knows exactly what associations or meanings are implied, but one thing is always for certain: situations are determined by one or several 'exteriors', 'antiforms' as Virilio described them. In this sense, the installation – and here the inflated term of installation is particularly appropriate – is a place in an experimental order where parameters are left undefined. And, as in medical or behavioural research, the parameters can only be reconstructed through tedious observation. The 'picture' becomes a surveillance monitor in the artistic study of a living object. As with Tony Oursler's installations, for example, Mik's are models of behaviour in specific situations taken from serious scenarios.

For Aernout Mik, the entire concrete location – that is, the video image, the installation space and the apparently devised behaviour of the actors – is very important. With this clearly delineated artistic framework – already clarified through the calculated specifications – he stamps out segments of content and form from the actually pre-determined space to create a thematic forum: in *Fluff* (1966), green and slimy clumps fly into the picture from an unknown source and land on wrapped furniture and stacks of palettes as well as lingering storeroom workers who are not in the least irritated by them. In *Piñata* (1999), discarded furniture and plastic squares are hurled from one video picture to another, where they are to be destroyed. *Blue Sinkhole* (1995) is a display of remarkably realistic attendants in a museum, where Mik's installation is also to be watched and guarded, such that the usual roles and perspectives are blurred. This is how Mik utilizes the versatility of the stage, but without creating a theatre.

The particular quality of Aernout Mik's artistic works consists not only of meddling with the layers of different levels of reality – which would mean abandoning control to chance – but also superimposing them on each other in such a way that their individual structures, purposes and meanings can be preserved. In *Kitchen* (1997), there are altogether five elderly men standing in a part of a small kitchenette, and each man continually finds a new reason to punch another. In doing so, he discovers pleasure, fun and seriousness, the consequences of real injury and losing, or the disquieting situation of 'two against one', of taking sides, Aernout Mik finds an interface at all levels at which the picture can be stopped and at every point a film with autonomous links emerges.

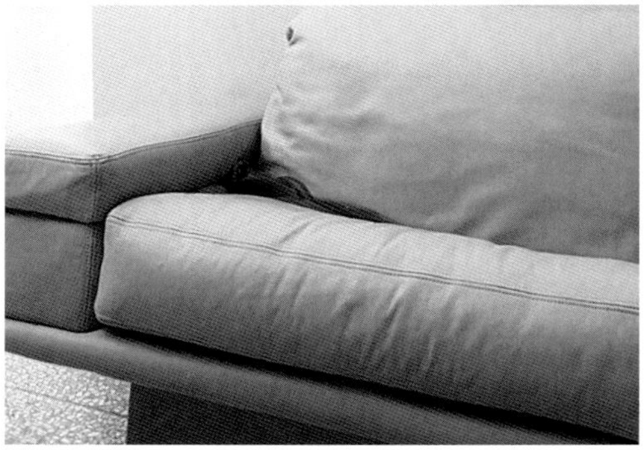

Modderbank, 1997, mixed media sculpture (detail)

Thus, the reason for the loop video trick is not a technical one, but has to do with creating a kind of 'running on the spot' at the point where systemic motions intersect. Mik achieves this by taking the content of the individual sequences and gently displacing them against each other by giving them different rhythmic phases. Previously shown sequences (which run between 15 and 20 minutes in length) are barely recognizable upon return, especially as the beginning and endings imperceptibly merge into each other. The nature of the repetition is as follows: one attempts the same things anew, in different ways. One essential element of this mode of working is that the imagined situation does not become a metaphor, that it does not freeze into a 'picture'. It must stay in motion so that its fundamental character, its virtues from which situations arise, evades depictions and is not lost.

As absurd as some moments in Aernout Mik's installations may be – for example one where black oil springs from between the cushions of a leather sofa in irregular rhythmic phases (Venice Biennial, 1997) – they are in no way related to Surrealist strategies. The point is not the subcutaneous and the subconscious. His experimental procedures are precisely considered and constructed. Nor are slapstick and big laughs his goals when three groups of three and four men play football with their trousers sewn together in *Mob* (1998). By the time the scene repeats itself, it is clear that the rules of the game are only the starting point, and from here the behavioural strategies, with their implications, are let loose. Like with Franz Erhard Walther, whose works are not comprised of the fabrics in his worksets but rather the uses of them, Aernout Mik's artistic work consists of reconstructing the presented situation's motifs and the observation of the viewer's constructed perception.

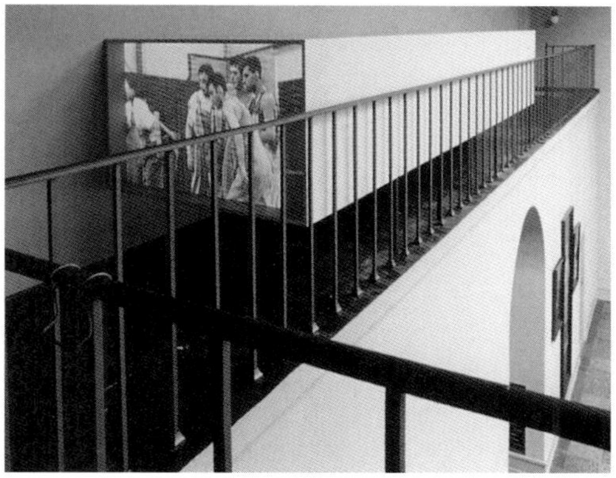

exhibition view 'Pictures for the Blue Room', Vigeland Museum, Oslo, 1998, **Mob**, 1998, video installation

In this respect, Mik's works differ essentially from the methods of collage and montage known today, for example, those of Raoul Hausmann or Robert Rauschenberg, because for him, rather than being a question of what aura of associations and meanings the pictures and signs convey, it is a question of their actual and determined structure. Mik's systemic view knows no hierarchies or value systems, only determining factors. Thus, a corresponding analytical coldness is found in his works which causes the isolated situations to appear so incredible. In *Swab* (1999), a man sits on the ground, his head full of blood. He is waiting (perhaps to be eventually treated by a doctor), but nothing happens. Meanwhile, as he and his body breathe heavily, somebody behind him rocks up and down in neat white sneakers (only the feet are visible). The injured man's concentration on what has happened to him makes the philosophy of 'functioning at this moment in time' a subject of his own perception and understanding, which, strangely enough, seems to even relieve him of his pain.

When I was a child, my mother strictly forbade me one childhood pleasure: to lie on my side and roll down a steep hill. Twisted guts, she prophesied, would be the consequence. Of course, I did not obey her orders and in fact did the exact opposite. It fascinated me to imagine my guts lying like loose tangles in my belly, becoming enmeshed from the brisk rolling. I tried to feel this and imagined – animated by my mother's prohibition – all my organs as separate parts in my body, just like my toy collection in their drawer. I discovered that I could shake the drawer and spill them onto the floor without being afraid of breaking or damaging anything. It merely resulted in another 'order', one which always became the starting point for a new game.

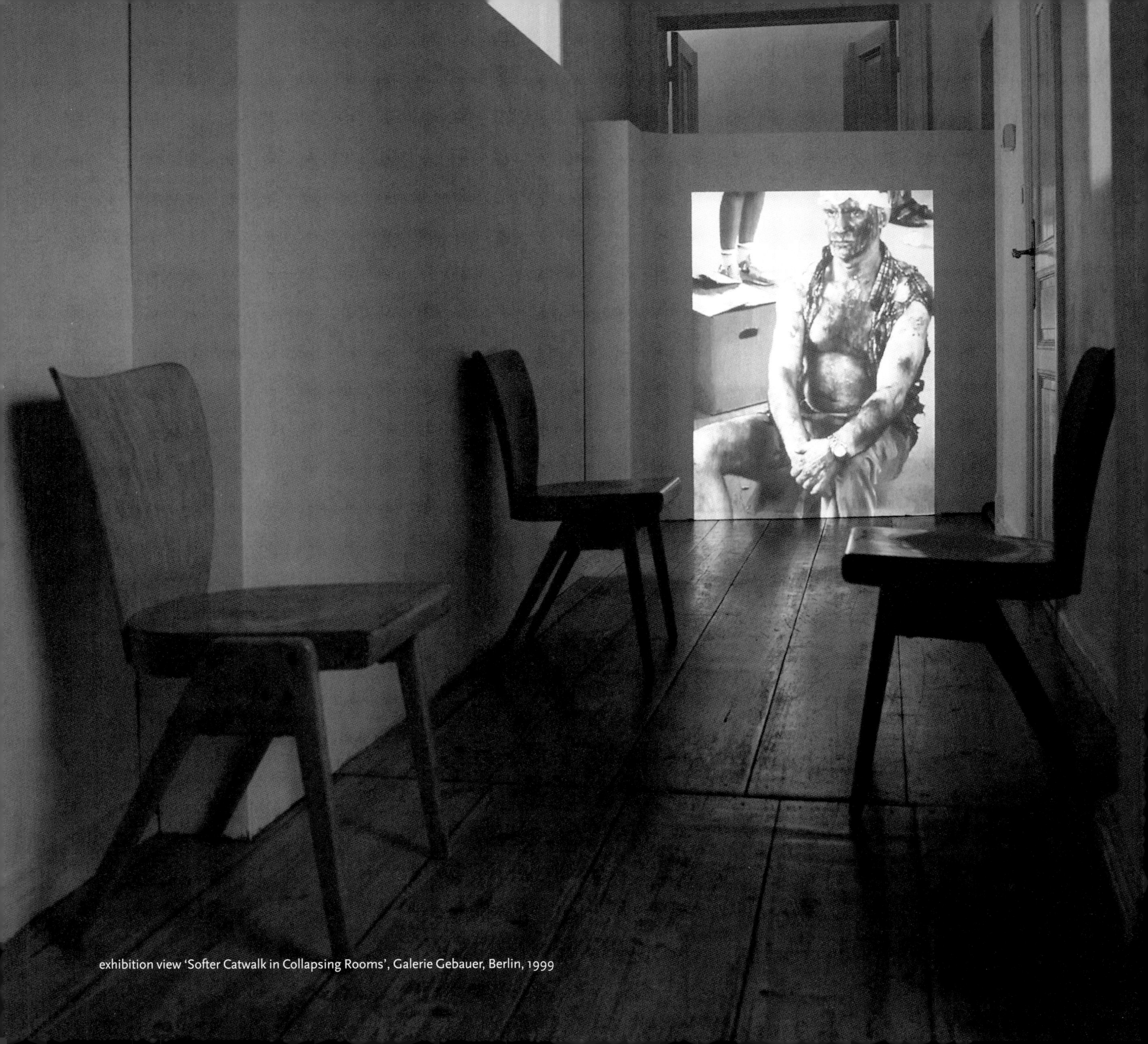

exhibition view 'Softer Catwalk in Collapsing Rooms', Galerie Gebauer, Berlin, 1999

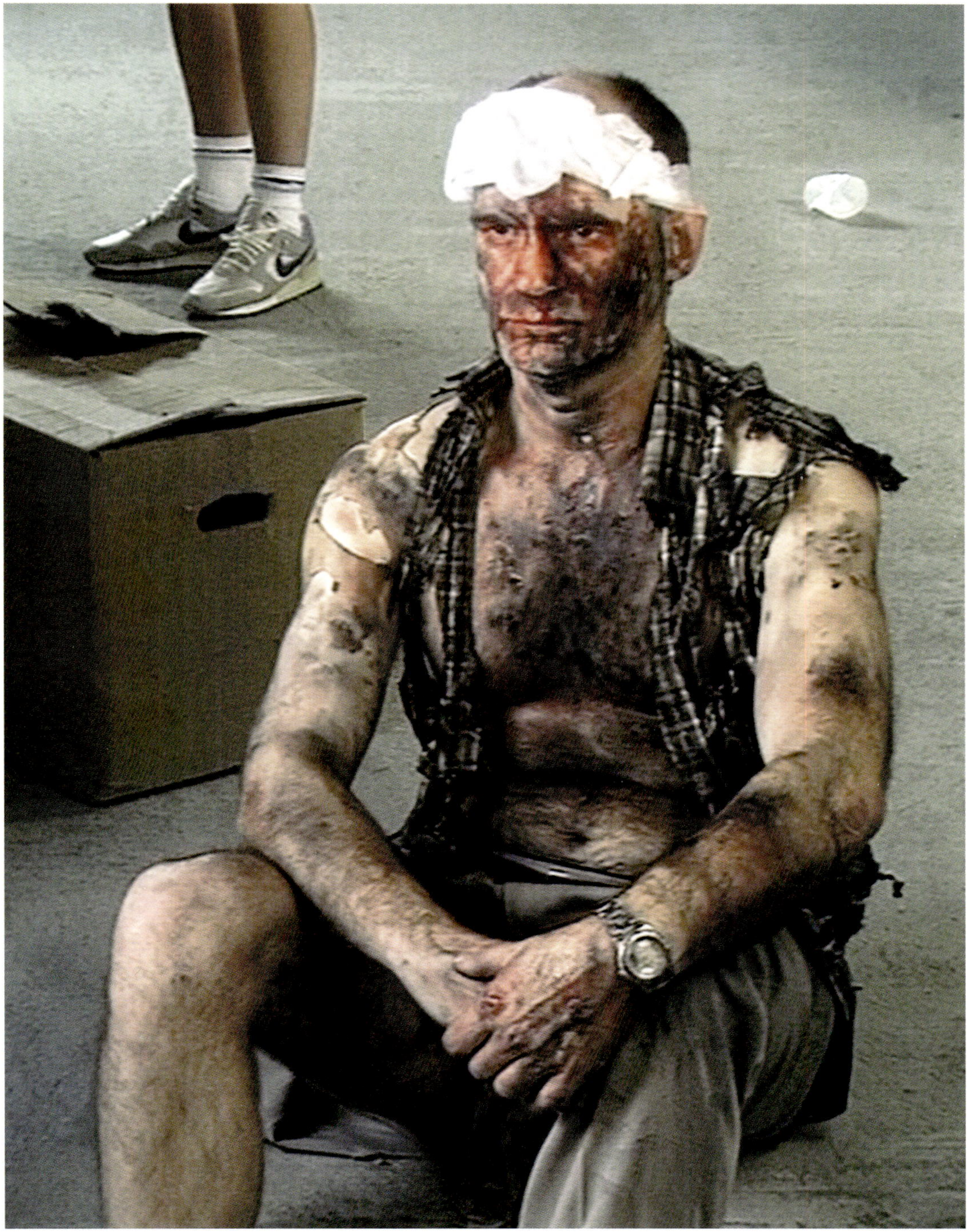

still from video installation **Swab**, 1999

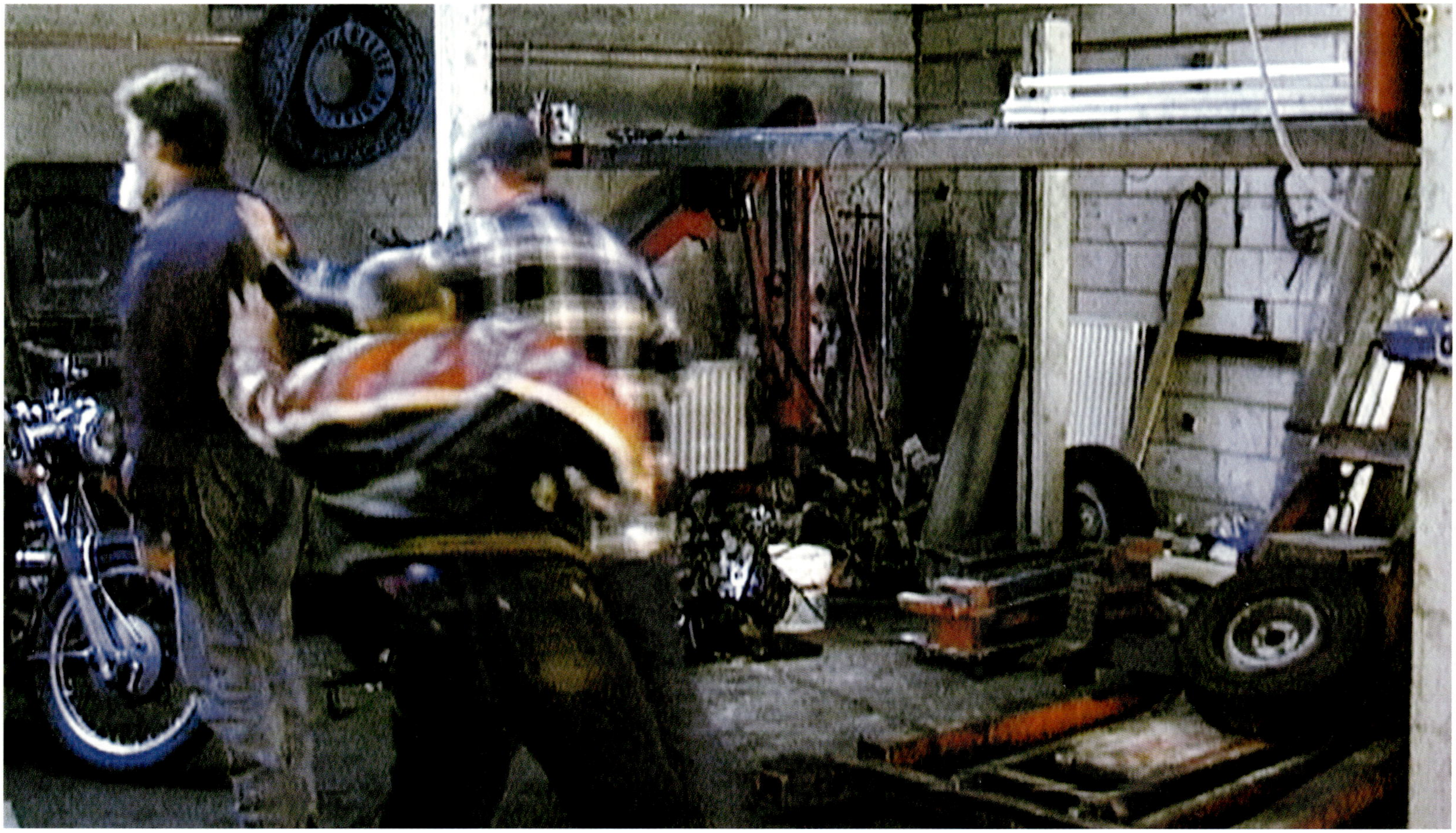

 stills from video installation **Garage**, 1998

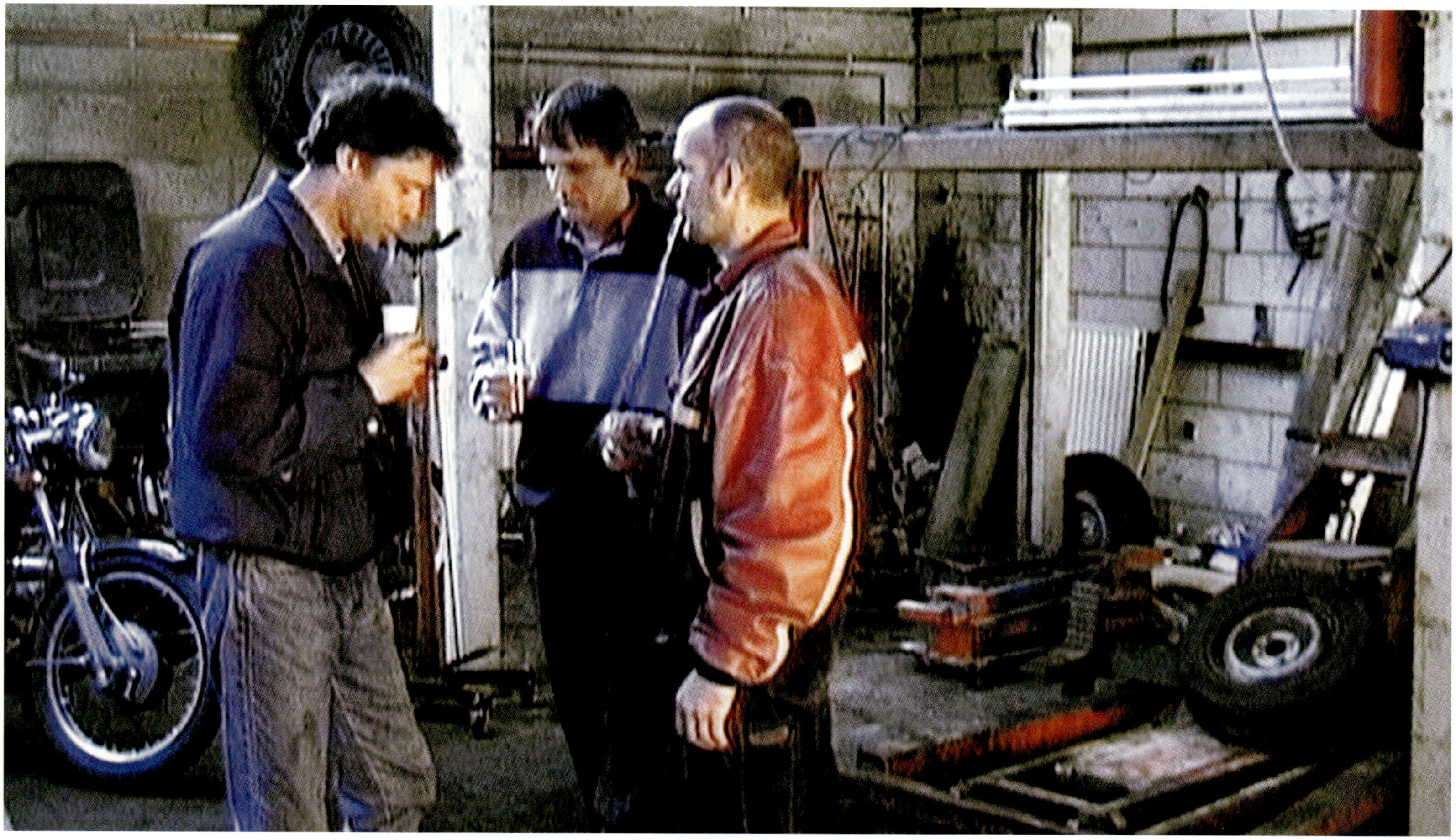

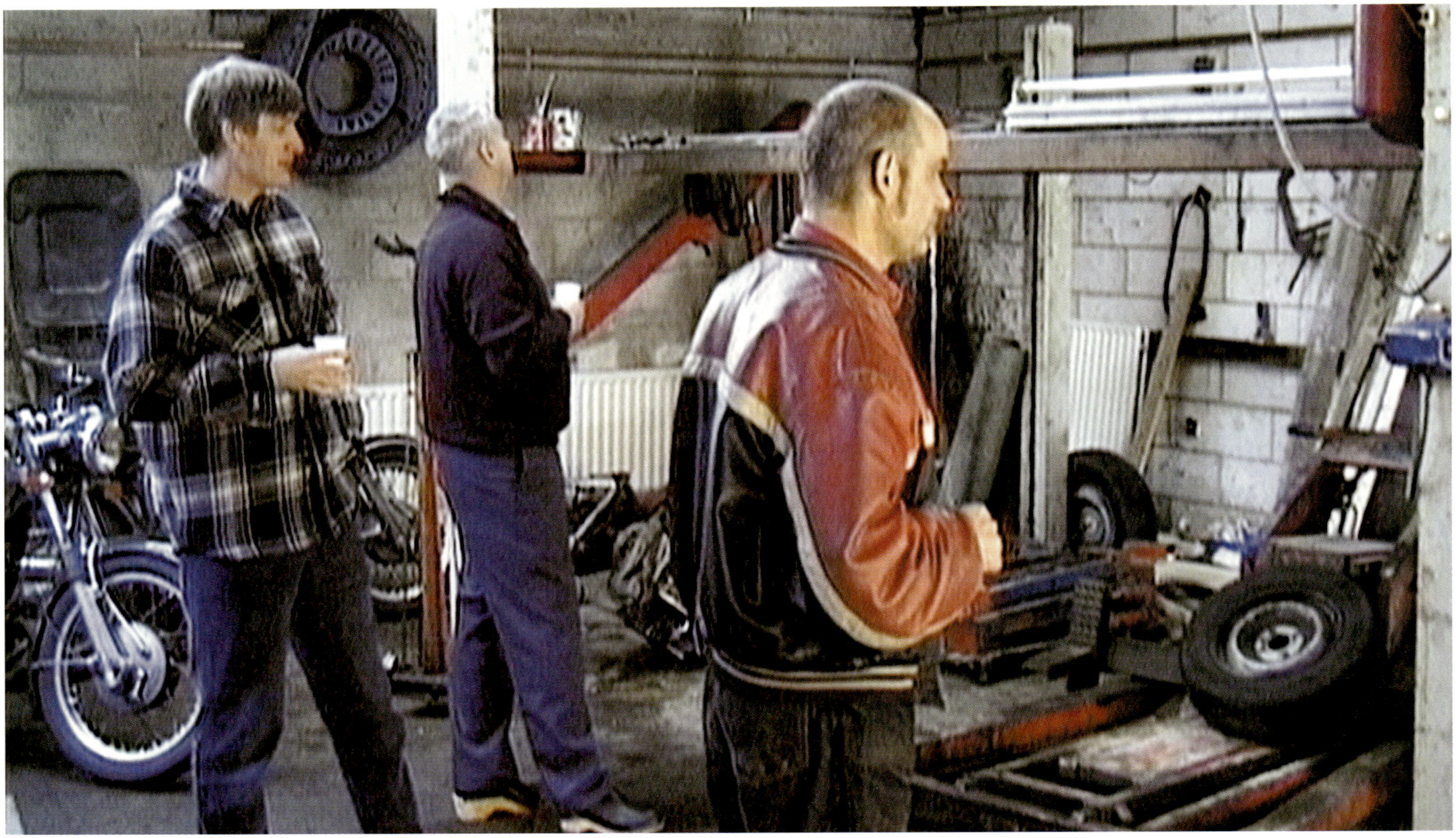

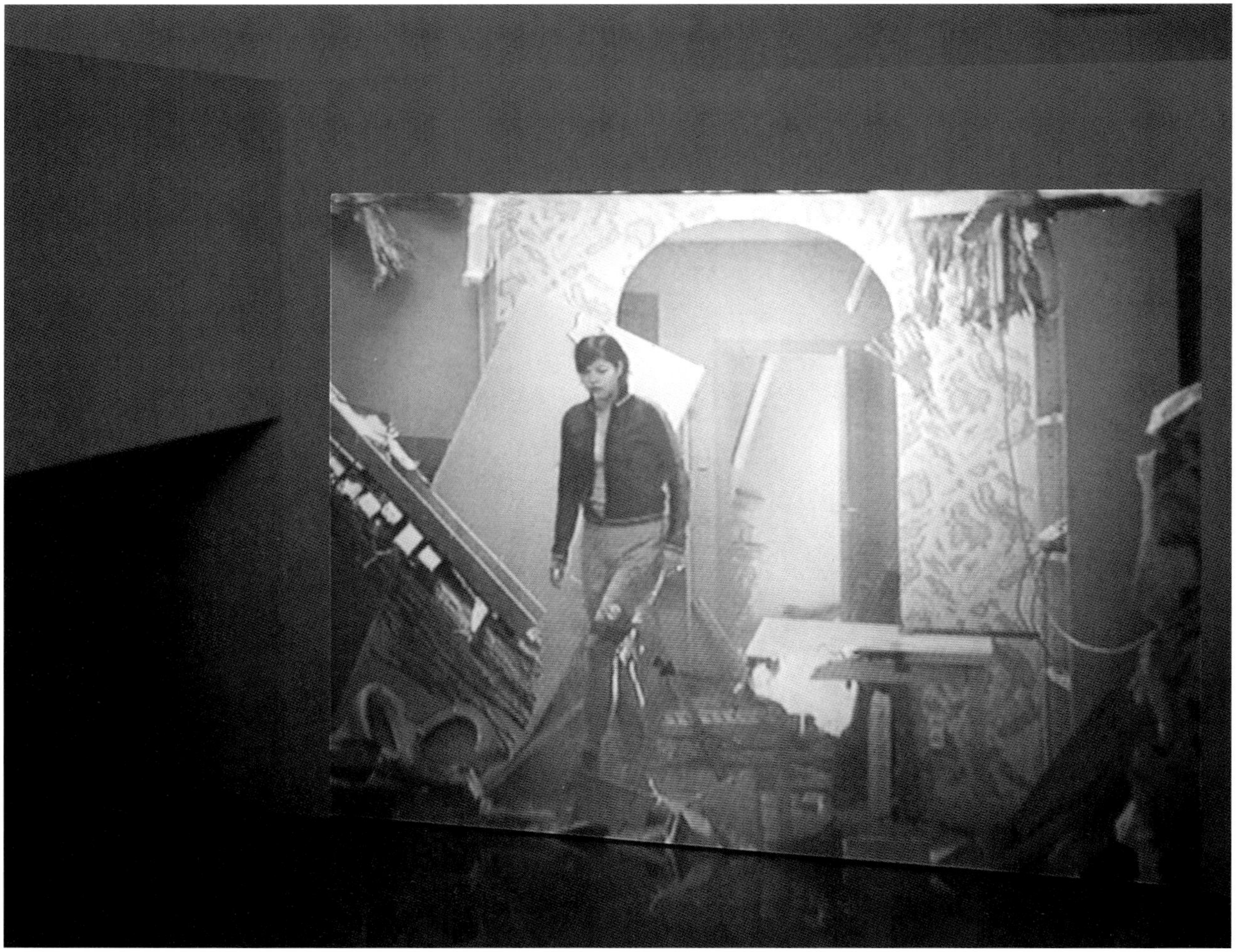

 exhibition view 'small disasters', Galerie Fons Welters, Amsterdam, 1999, **Softer Catwalk in Collapsing Rooms**, 1999, video installation

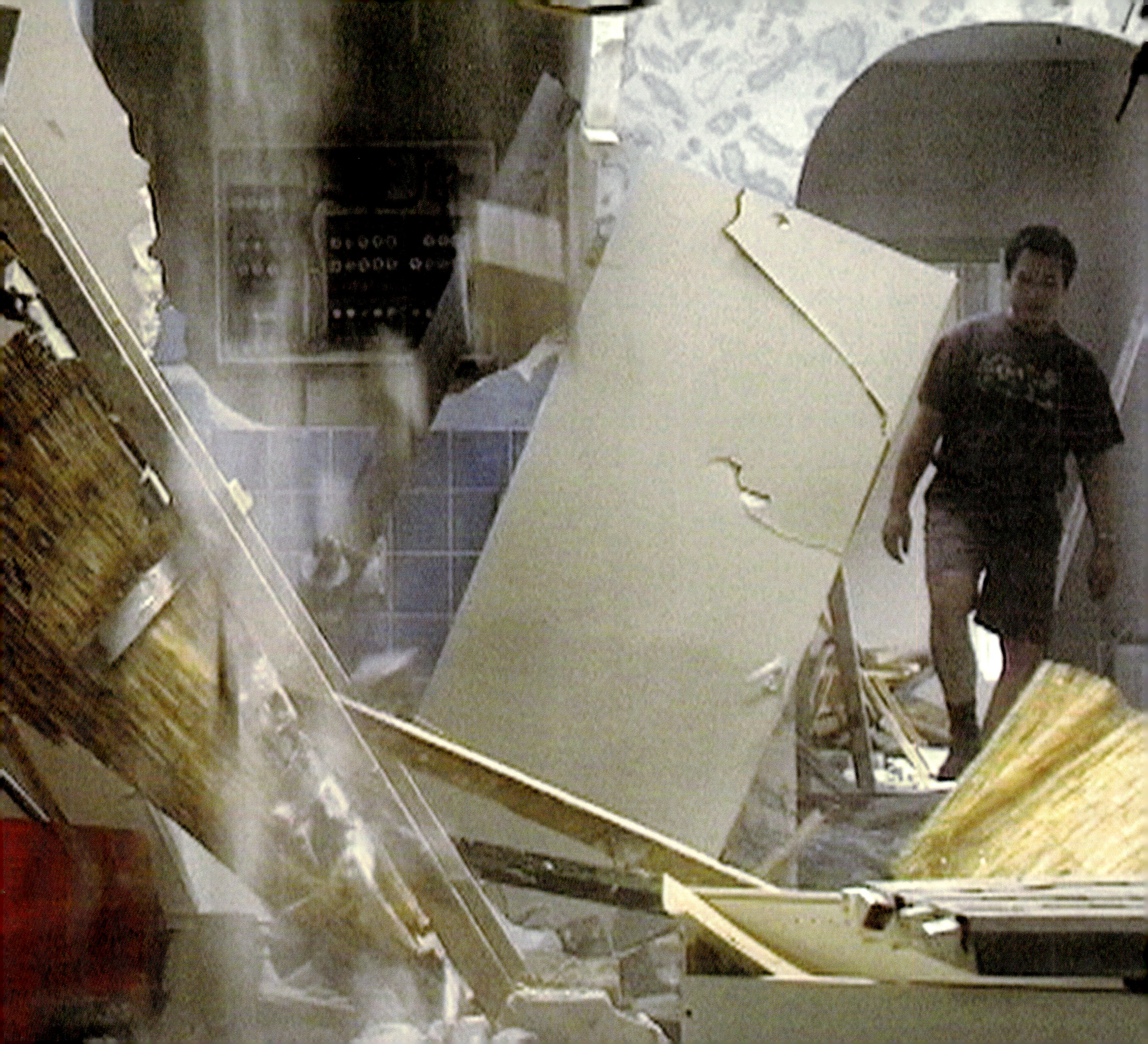

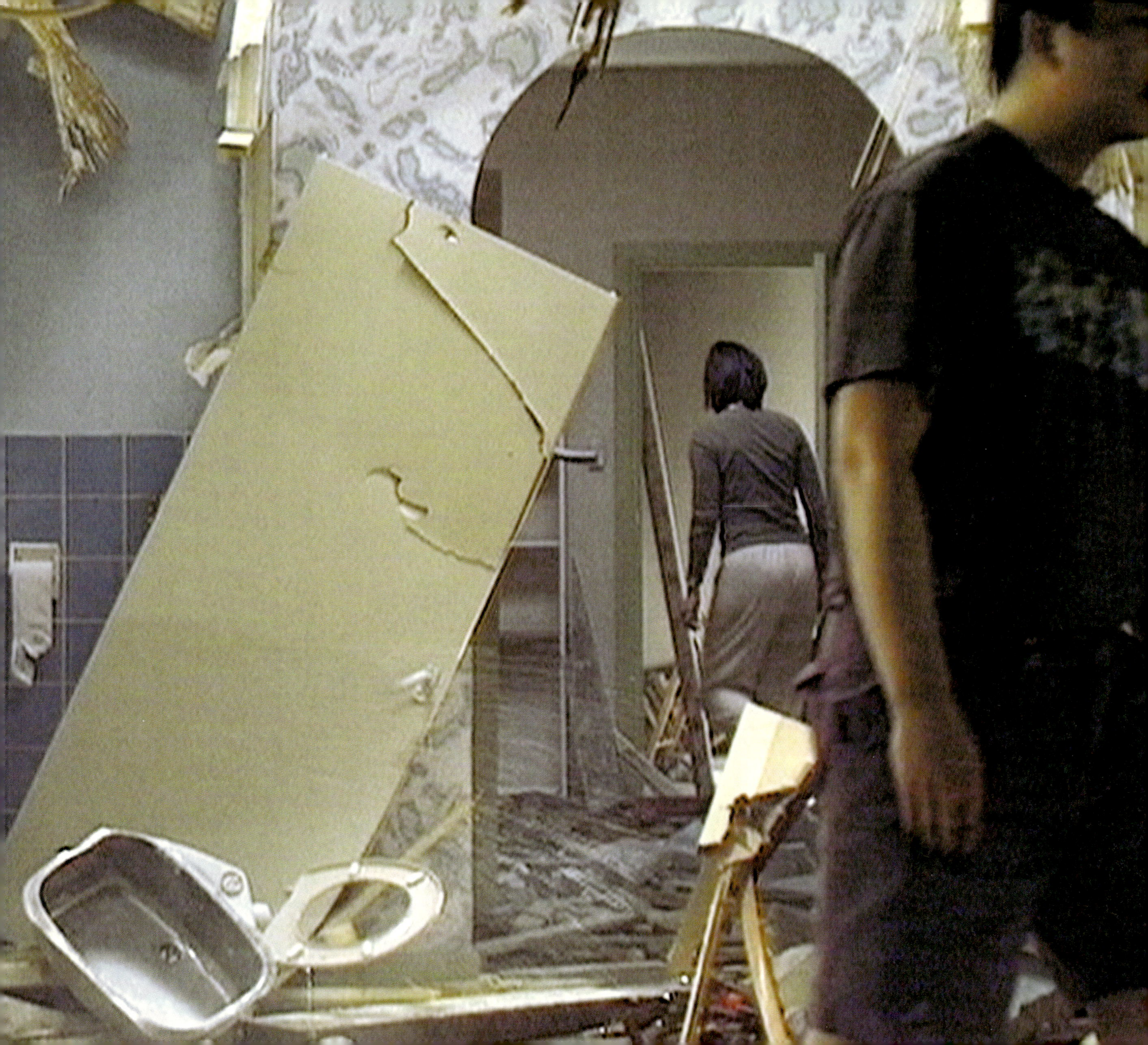

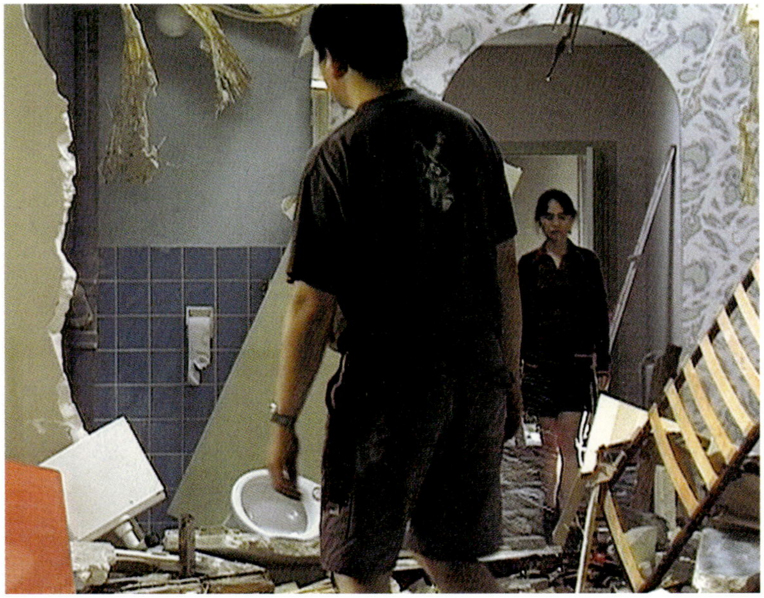

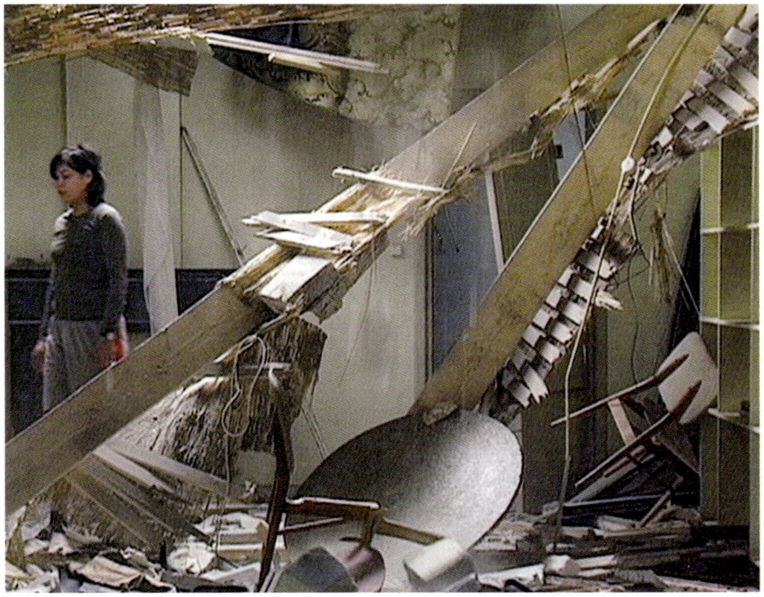

stills from video installation **Softer Catwalk in Collapsing Rooms**, 1999

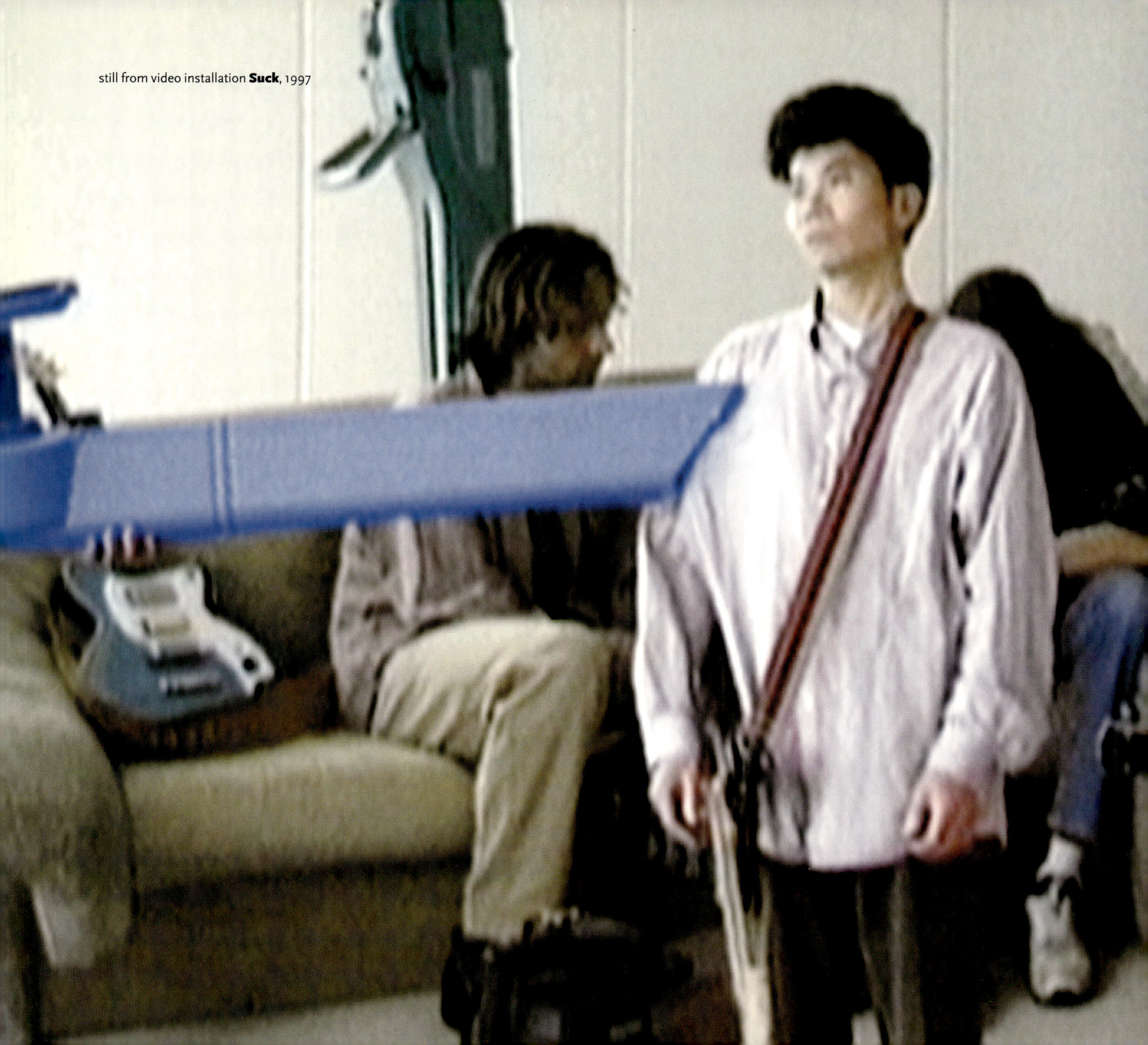

still from video installation **Suck**, 1997

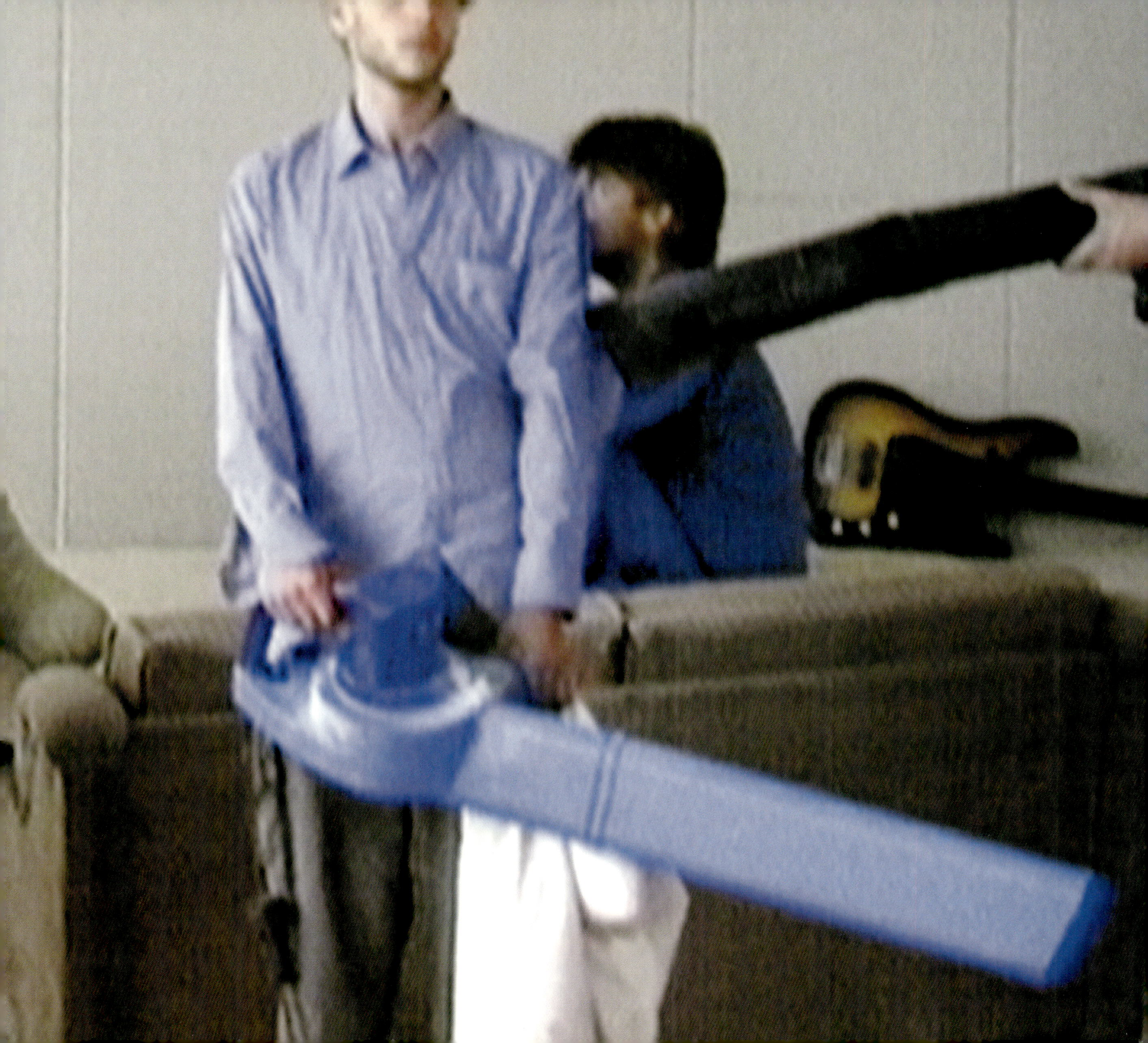

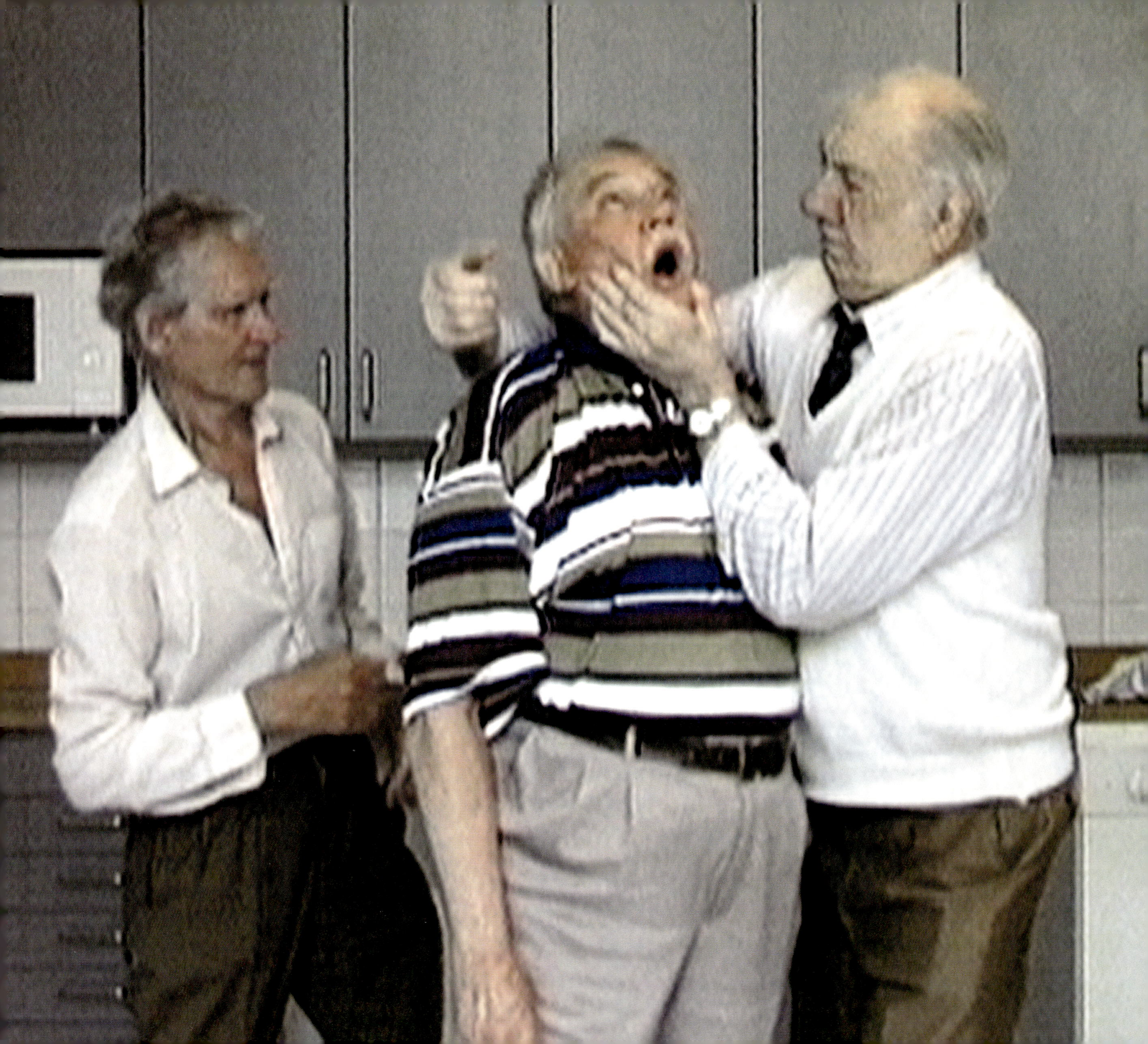

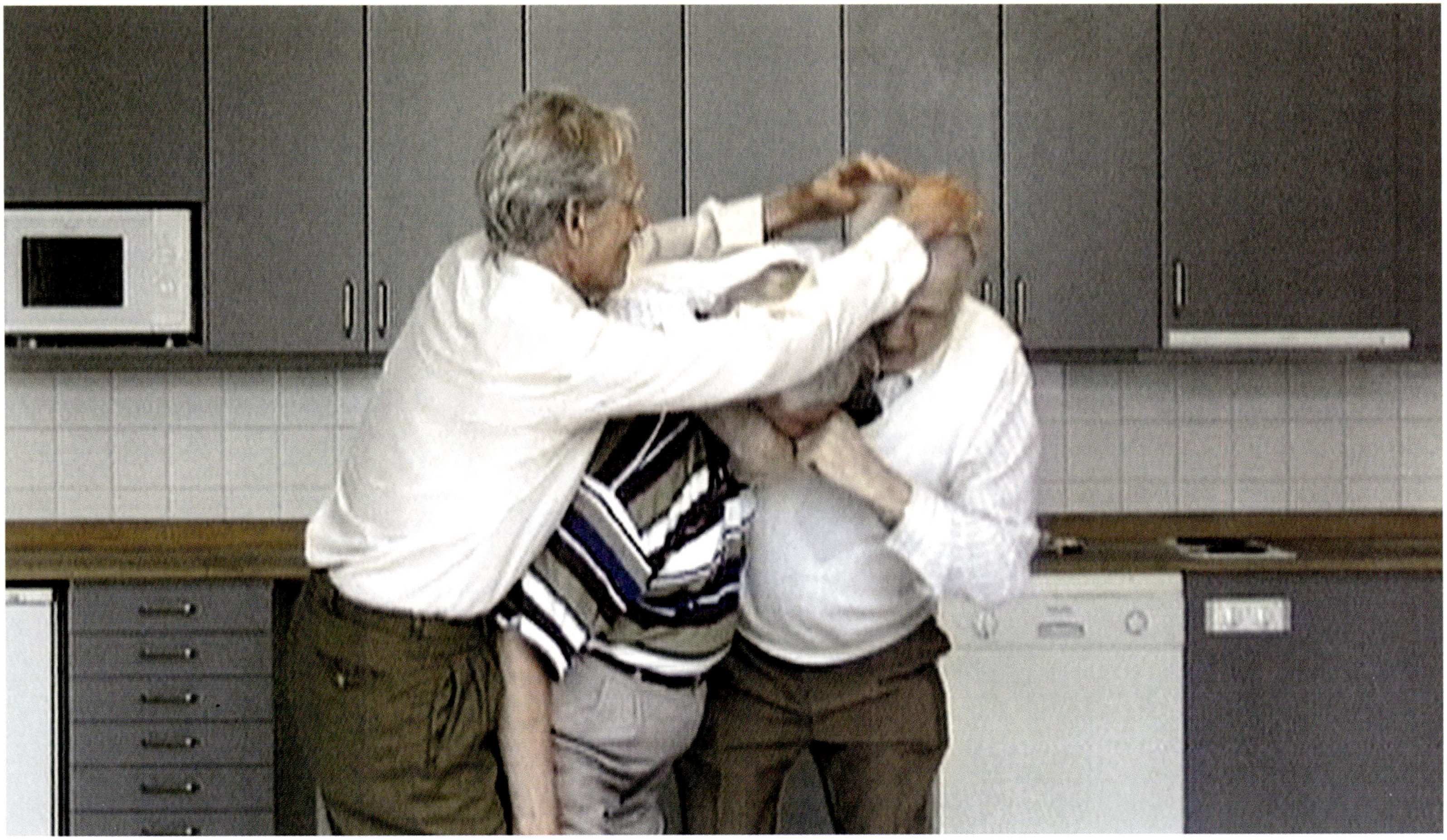

stills from video installation **Kitchen**, 1997

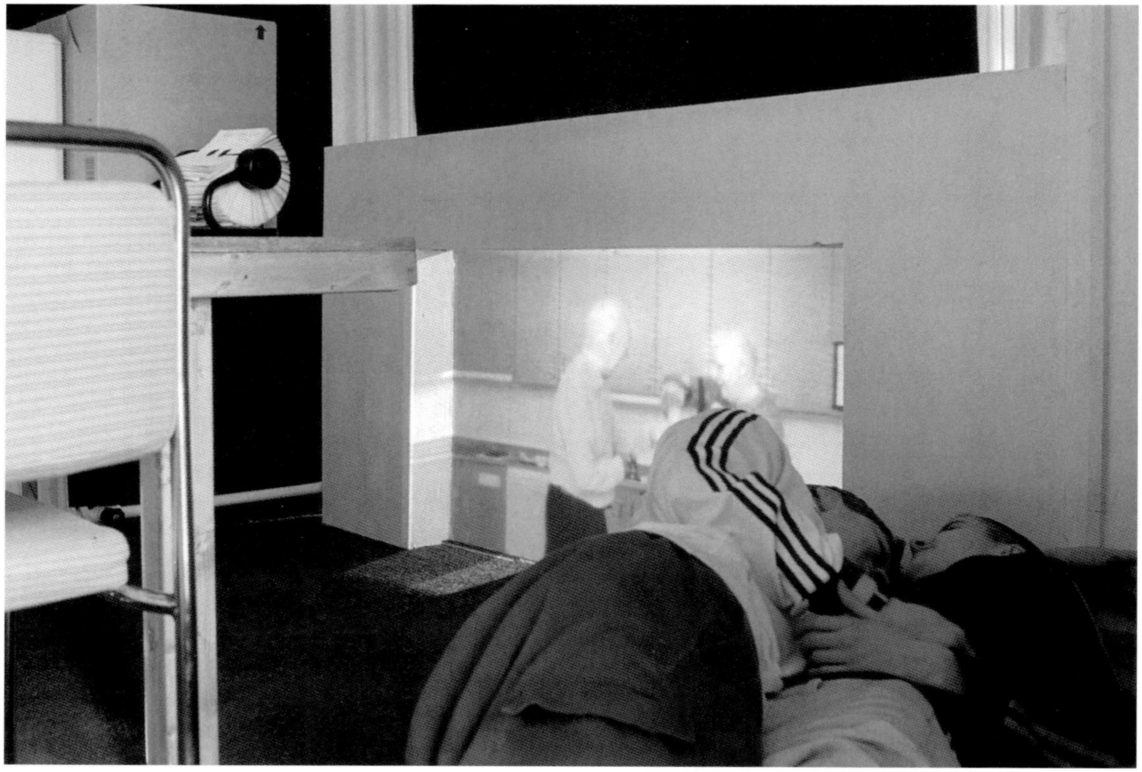

exhibition view 'A Place to Be', Büro Friedrich, Berlin 1997, **Kitchen**, 1997, video installation

Behavioural Fossils

Tijs Goldschmidt

Two old men are fighting in a spotless kitchen. Neat wall cupboards, sink unit, built-in oven, washing up machine: design. A tea-towel is lying on top of the cupboard, as if it has fled from the fight. Lying down at a safe distance, he watches. It could be the kitchen in an old people's home. Perhaps this is the first scuffle in this brand-new kitchen? The old men are not really fighting, though. It is not serious. You realise that after only a few seconds of Aernout Mik's video *Kitchen*.

It is a comical sight, because the two old men are mainly shadow-boxing, teasing one another. They flail their arms slowly through the air, throw their arms around one another, break loose and carry on fighting. One is short and fat, the other tall and thin. They change roles regularly. At one moment the short and fat one attacks, at another the tall and thin one. The old men are playing, and the expressions on their faces confirm that. The mouth slightly open, teeth covered by the upper lip. They both present a face at play, a facial expression that you also see on chimpanzees at play.

Play is by definition not the real thing, but the play of these old men is even less the real thing than just lacking in seriousness. It makes a very artificial impression. That is partly because playing is practising for later, while we know that these men do not have much later to look forward to. The artificiality lies mainly in the fact that these men play much less roughly than young boys do. And yet that was one of the instructions that Mik gave his real-life actors: imagine you are back in the school yard and behave as if you are fighting.

A later shot shows two other old men shadow-boxing. A short, wiry figure, who makes the same lively impression as the men in the first shot, and a tall, impotent man, fragile as a sponge finger. After a couple of minutes you already feel that you can place these four men. The fact that you have that feeling already says something about the function of play. I am an adult viewer and my period of educational play is a long way behind me. Play is learning to assess who you are up against, and the viewer of this video involuntarily joins the shadow-boxers in making assessments.

The small, wiry man is almost constantly on the attack. You wonder whether he is not taking it seriously, because although he does not follow through the punches, there is nothing playful about his face. He keep his lips firmly pressed together. At any rate, he is clearly in his element in this role. A basher. And before you realise it you are rewinding his life and interpreting it. You imagine that he has played that attacking role before. You see that boy fighting and provoking others, even if it was more than sixty years ago.

Regular role exchange is a strong indication that two mammals are playing, but it is not always easy to draw the line between play and seriousness. The impotent man puts on a playing face now and then, although you do not have the impression that he is enjoying it very much. Most of the time he is defending himself, warding off blows, and ducking his opponent's shadow-boxing. He makes a vulnerable impression, and has a painful expression on his face when his ear-lobes are playfully tugged. He attacks now and then, but you can hardly call his attacking movements punches. They have no force behind them, and even turn into endearing stroking movements on his rival's cheek. You can imagine him in the school yard too. An outsider. A trained loser. I would not be surprised if he had been systematically bullied and on the losing end throughout childhood.

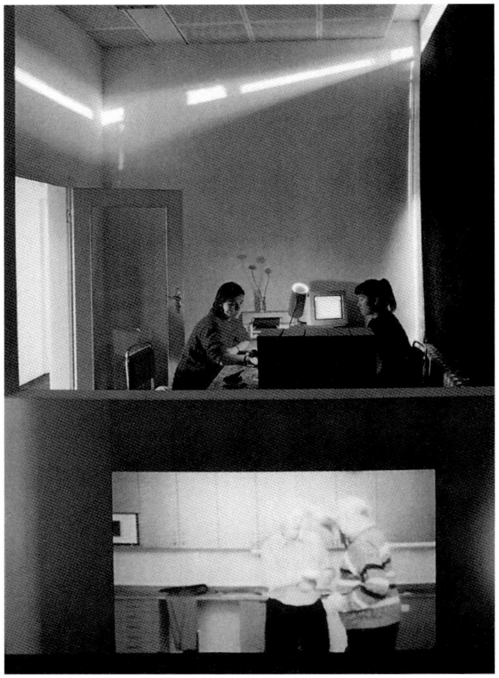

exhibition view 'A Place to Be', Büro Friedrich, Berlin 1997, **Kitchen**, 1997, video installation

This fragile man has produced a very different collection of behavioural fossils than the basher, thanks to Mik's instructions. It is a collection that is also very different from the movements of the men in the first shot, who acted as if they had been aroused from their slumbers. Has the sponge finger been given a life sentence? Just as you never forget how to swim, this man has never forgotten how to lose. As a viewer, you immediately feel sympathy for him and have the urge to lend him a hand in that school yard. But you know that you are more than sixty years too late, and besides that cheerful fat figure comes dancing into the picture.

Not only does he deliver mock punches, but he comes in for his share too, as if he keeps getting pounded by enormous blows. That is not the case. He plays with enthusiasm and seems to be enjoying himself, but he too is doing something *serious*. Without any hesitation he immediately sides with the basher instead of defending the fragile man. They form a coalition and take him on together. It is difficult to say whether this is their first joint venture.

Playing faces, two men who form an alliance to attack a third. Absence of playing faces. And then an old man with a moustache puts in his first appearance and spontaneously intervenes. He separates the two shadow-boxers in front of the sink unit. Stop fighting, lads! This behaviour can all be seen, cutting through the staged appearances. Real and artificial behaviour interlock in a remarkable way. There is no sound, so that the mood of the film comes to resemble a dream. The fact that there is a story to hang on to contributes to this. These could be scuffles that are still being acted out in a dream. Before waking, and thus before their narration. But I am awake, aren't I? That feels strange too.

The protagonist in the novel *Ferdydurke* by the Polish writer Witold Gombrowicz (1904-1969) is called Jozef. Jozef is thirty years old, but he becomes a child again because the people around him treat him as a child. He even feels that he is possessed by a demon that tempts him to commit childish behaviour. When he is in adult company, Jozef feels like an adolescent imitating adults. He is reluctant to stop being a kid, but he is well aware of the need to be transformed into an adult. One of the people who treat Jozef as a child is a certain Professor T. Pimko, a schoolmaster who wants to reduce Jozef to size. 'The big reducer' Pimko lets Jozef, Josje from now on, loose among a group of adolescents in a school yard. Pimko follows his bizarre experiment closely. He is hidden behind an oak and observes the behaviour of the children and the alarmingly shrunken adult in the yard. The lads soon realise that there is something strange about their new classmate.

Kitchen could be seen as a visual variant of Gombrowicz's story. Old men who revert to the role that they played more than sixty years before in the school yard. Old people often think that their youth is gone for ever, but if you see this video, you begin to wonder whether they are right. A couple of simple director's instructions work as a trigger and bring out the 'secret immaturity' that is hidden inside everybody. Each of these men takes off his mask and plays his old role to perfection. The resurrection of schoolboys in a bunch of old men. Gombrowicz would probably not have been surprised by this Lazarus effect, but I was surprised. It reminded me of something that happened with the chimpanzees in Burgers Zoo in Arnhem.

A group of several dozen chimpanzees live there in semi-natural conditions. The chimpanzees spend the day out of doors on a sloping terrain surrounded by a moat. At the end of the afternoon they go to their night quarters. In their natural habitat, chimpanzees live in groups of several dozen to a hundred or so individuals. They go around in constantly changing groups. Unlike the situation on the chimpanzee island, which is one hectare in size, in nature the whole group is never together at the same time. The males remain loyal to the group all their lives, while the females transfer from one group to another now and then. It is the males with their group loyalty who are constantly involved in a struggle for power, for which the support of the females is essential.

In 1983 Bert Haanstra made the film *Chimps onder elkaar* (Chimps together) of the group in Burgers Zoo. The leader Nikkie was the star of that film, but it was to be his last – he died soon after making the film. Yeroen and Dandy, the two other adult males, soon became arch rivals. More than a year later, on an evening in 1985, a fragment of the film was projected in the shadowy quarters where the chimpanzees spend the winter. Haanstra and the ethologist Otto Adang wanted to know whether the chimpanzees would react to the film. Is a chimpanzee able to recognise himself or other chimpanzees in a film more than a year later? The introduction to the film, dealing with the background to the experiment, was skipped because it was supposed that the chimpanzees would be bored by it. The projection started with footage of their own behaviour. From the very first moment the chimpanzees watched in concentration as the film was projected onto the cream-coloured wall. Like Mik's videos, the film was projected without sound. It was absolutely quiet in the room, but the chimpanzees were clearly excited. The hair stood on end on some of them. When an adolescent in the film irritated one of the females by throwing a stick in her direction, the female chimpanzees in the audience expressed their disapproval. But it was anybody's guess whether the audience also recognised which female from the group was being pestered and by whom.

Adang is convinced that the dead leader Nikkie was recognised when he appeared soon afterwards in a close-up shot. His hair stood on end and he pumped himself up in an act of

aggrandizement. At this Dandy began to scream with his mouth wide open and his teeth bared. He turned round and walked straight towards his arch enemy Yeroen. Then he threw an arm around Yeroen's shoulders and climbed into his lap, exactly as he would have done in a comparable situation when Nikkie was still alive, when he would have climbed into the lap of his old ally Yeroen too. Yeroen did not scream, but smiled hesitantly with his teeth bared. He remained fixated on the picture and put his arm around Dandy. The apparition of Nikkie had immediately thrown Dandy and Yeroen back into their old roles. The rest of the chimpanzees had no time to pay any attention to the striking reactions of the two adult males. They continued to stare at the film. He is back! That is what they must have thought in their chimpanzee minds.
If Gombrowicz and his pornographic gaze had been present at the screening of this film, he would have paid more attention than the ethologists to the reactions of the chimpanzee audience. At least, that is what I would expect. And if he had been unable to attend, he would have sent Professor T. Pimko to take notes on the excited chimpanzees in the dusky cinema. If Aernout Mik had been invited to this showing of the film, he would no doubt have filmed the reactions of the chimpanzee audience to the film. The relations of power have changed so profoundly in the meantime that for the time being there is no point in repeating the experiment. All the same, I would give a lot to see the filmed reactions of chimpanzees to a film about their own past. Because behavioural fossils can be conjured up from chimpanzees too.

Sources
Chimpanzee politics, Frans de Waal, Harper & Row, New York 1982 (new edition: Johns Hopkins University Press, Baltimore, 1998).

De machtigste chimpansee van Nederland [The most powerful chimpanzee in the Netherlands], Otto Adang, Marlou Wijsman, Uitgeverij Nieuwezijds, Amsterdam 1999.

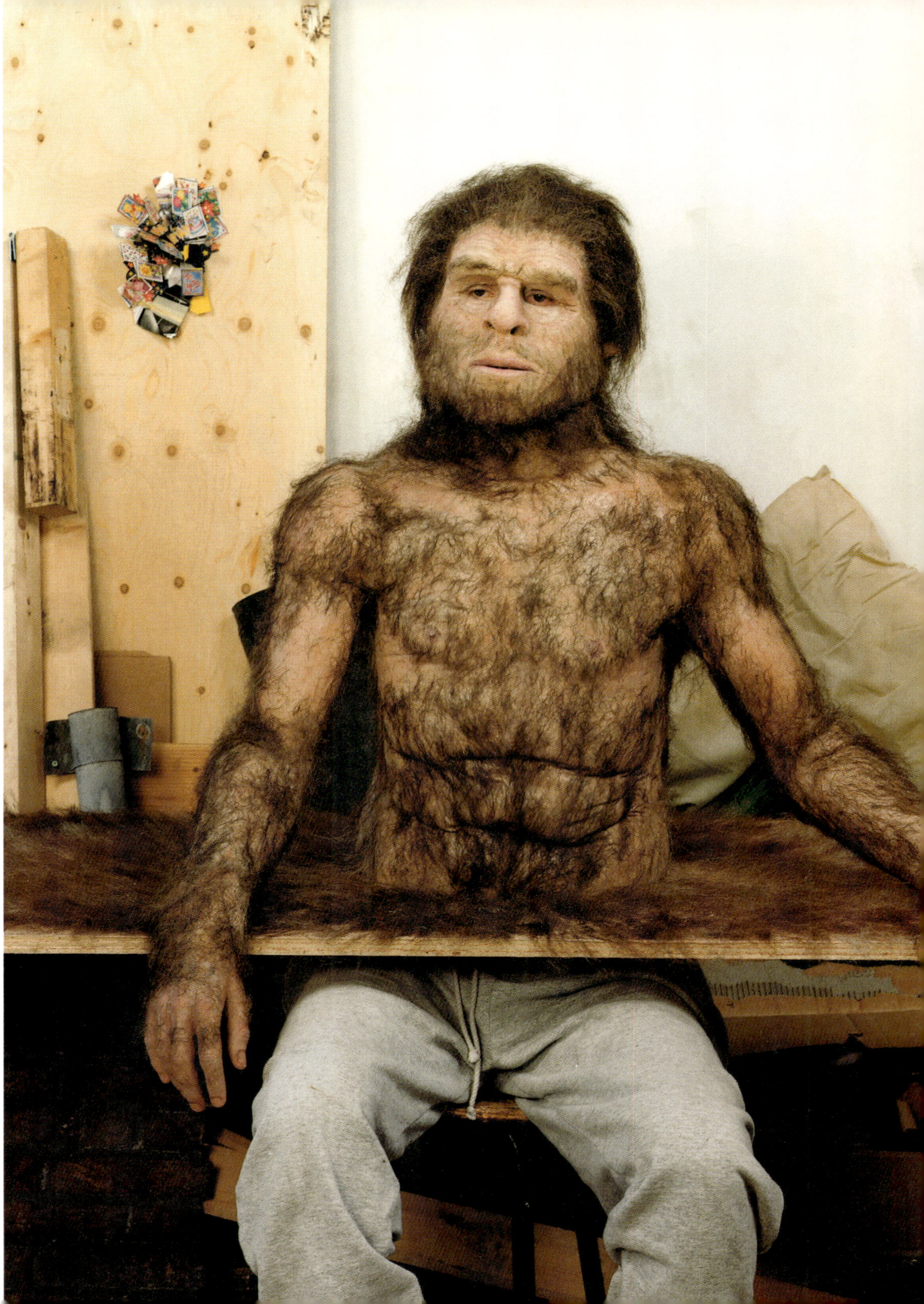

Portrait, 1998, colour photograph on aluminium

exhibition view 'Hongkongoria', Stedelijk Van Abbemuseum, Eindhoven, 1998, **Hongkongoria**, 1997-1998, Marjoleine Boonstra and Aernout Mik, 7 screen video installation

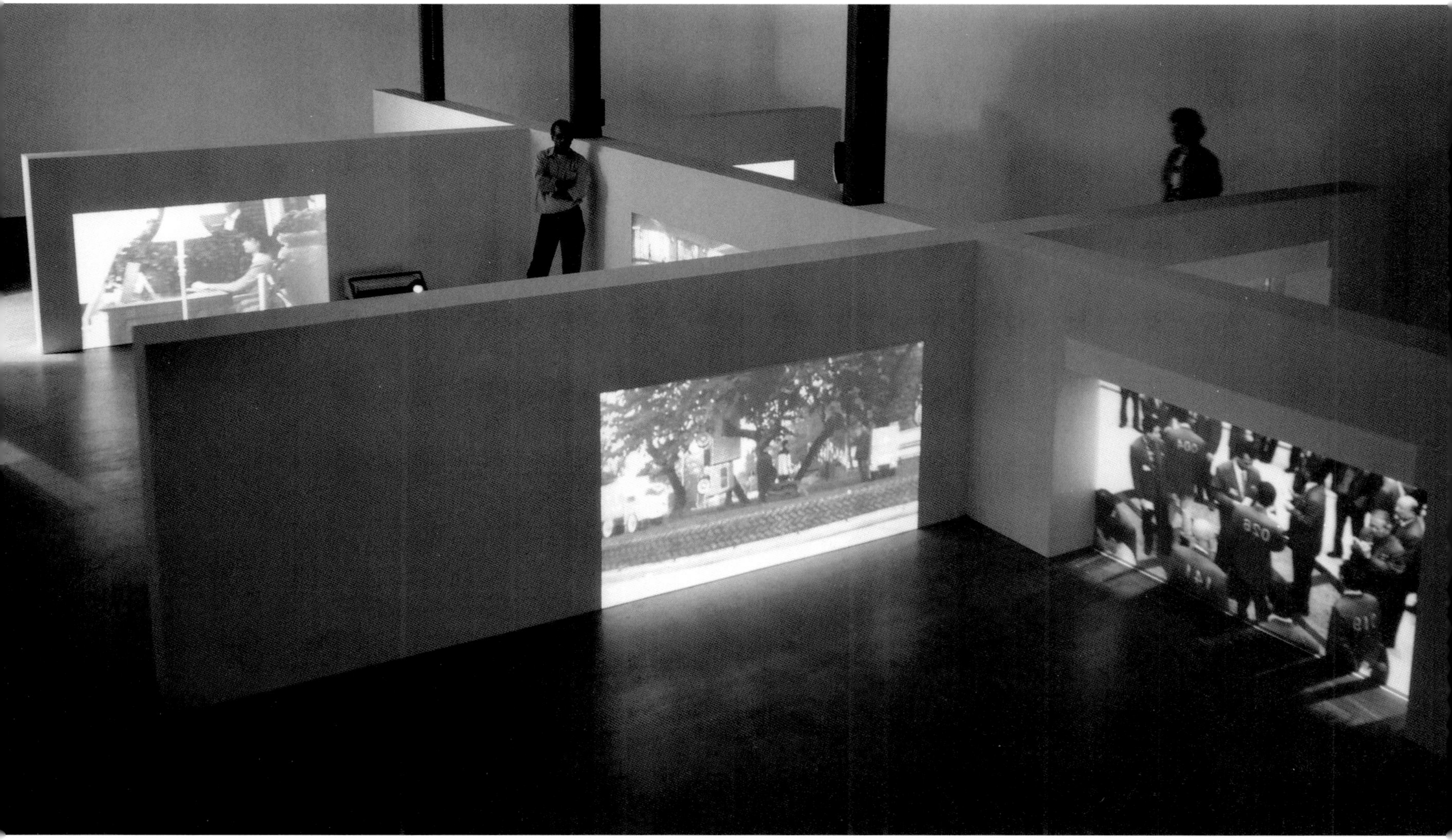

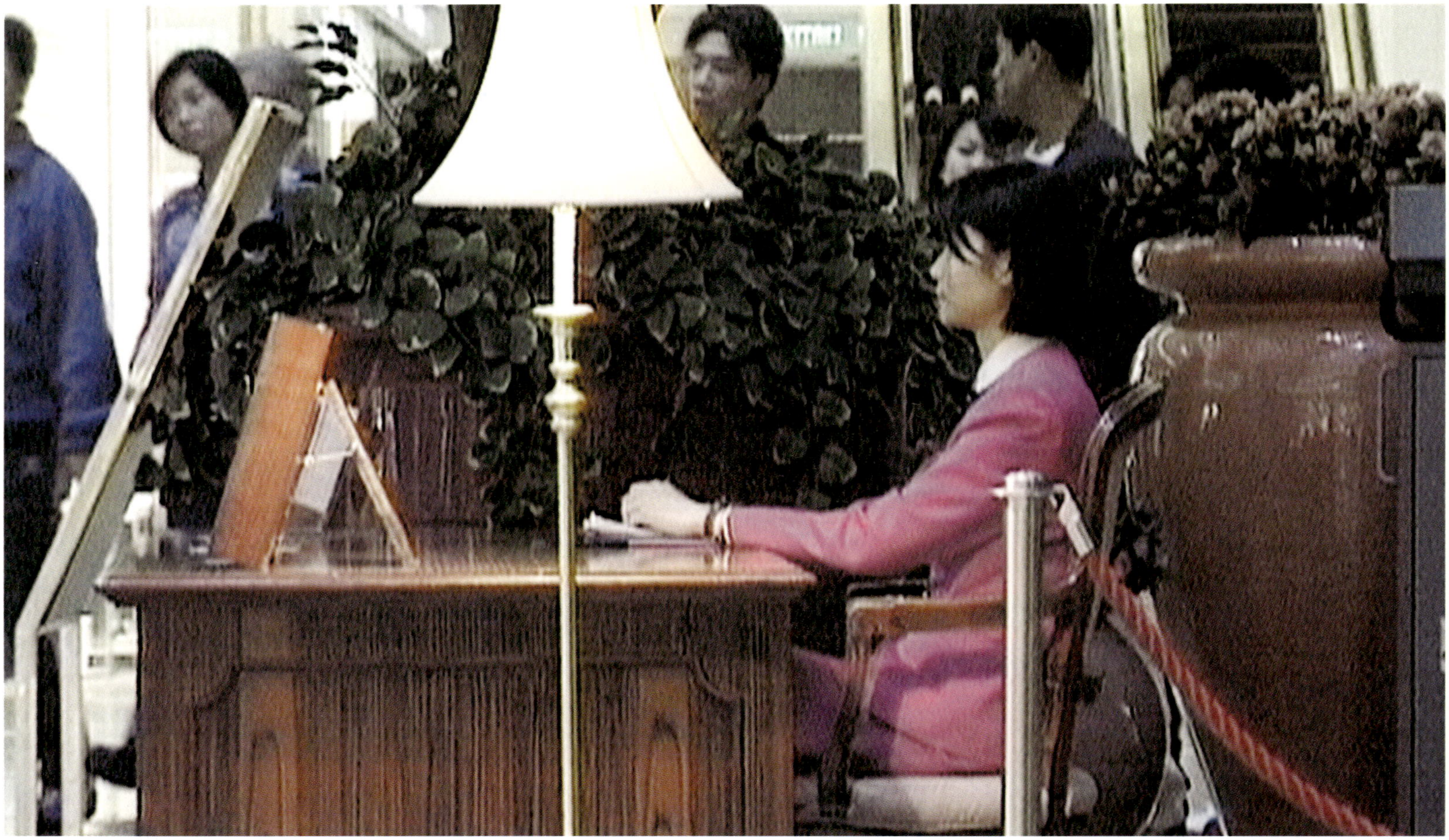

 stills from video installation **Hongkongoria**, 1997-1998

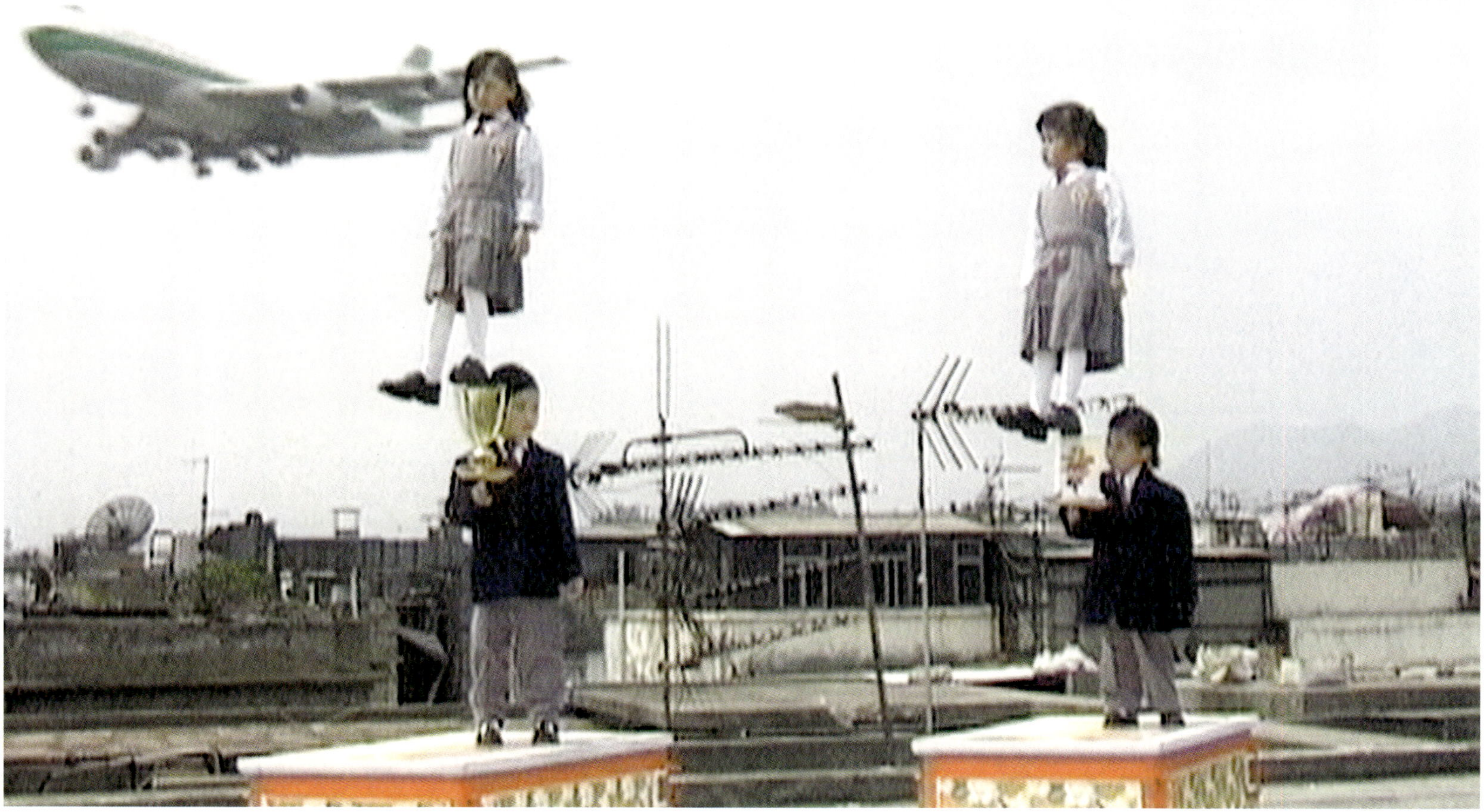

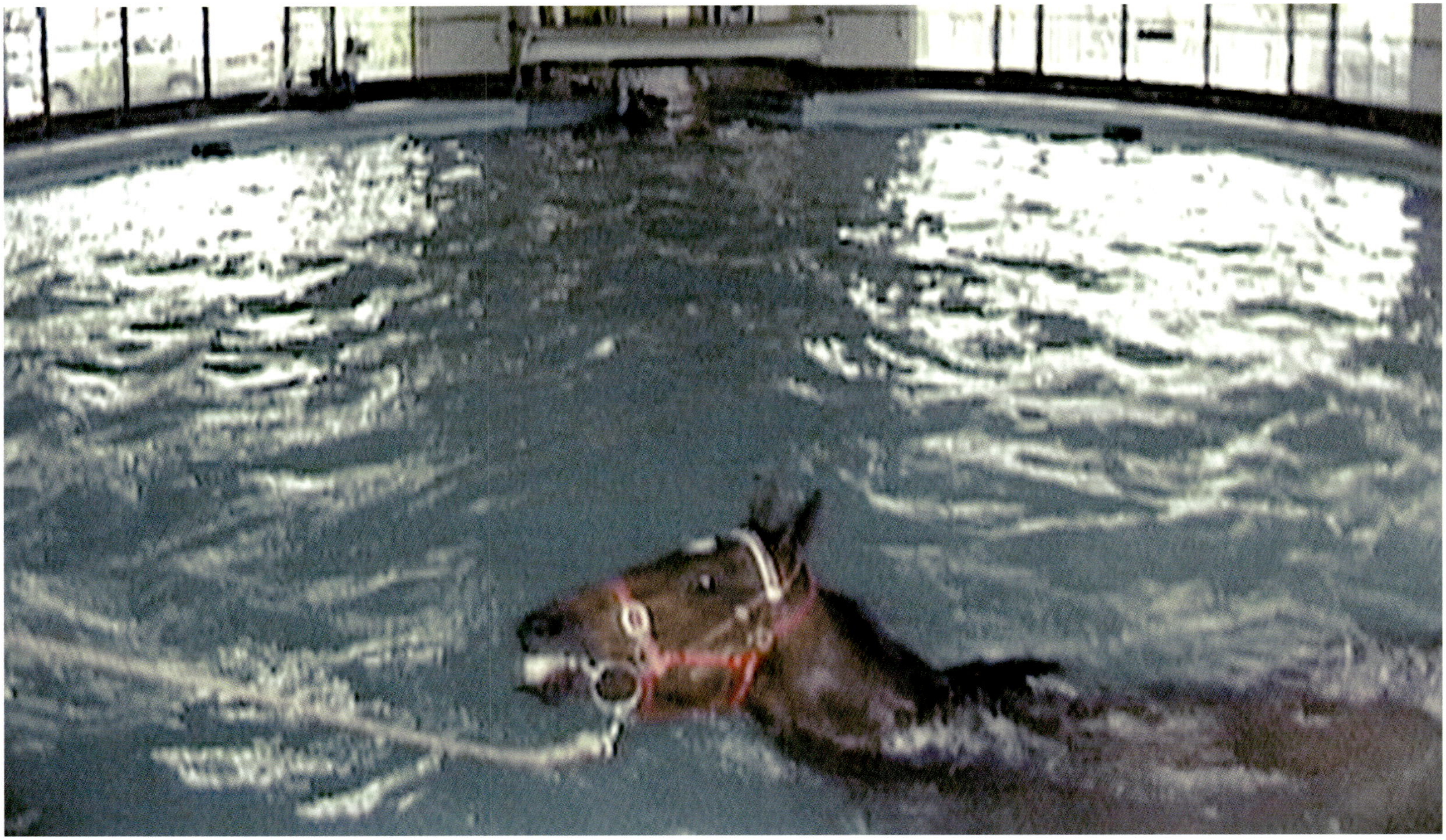

 stills from video installation **Hongkongoria**, 1997-1998

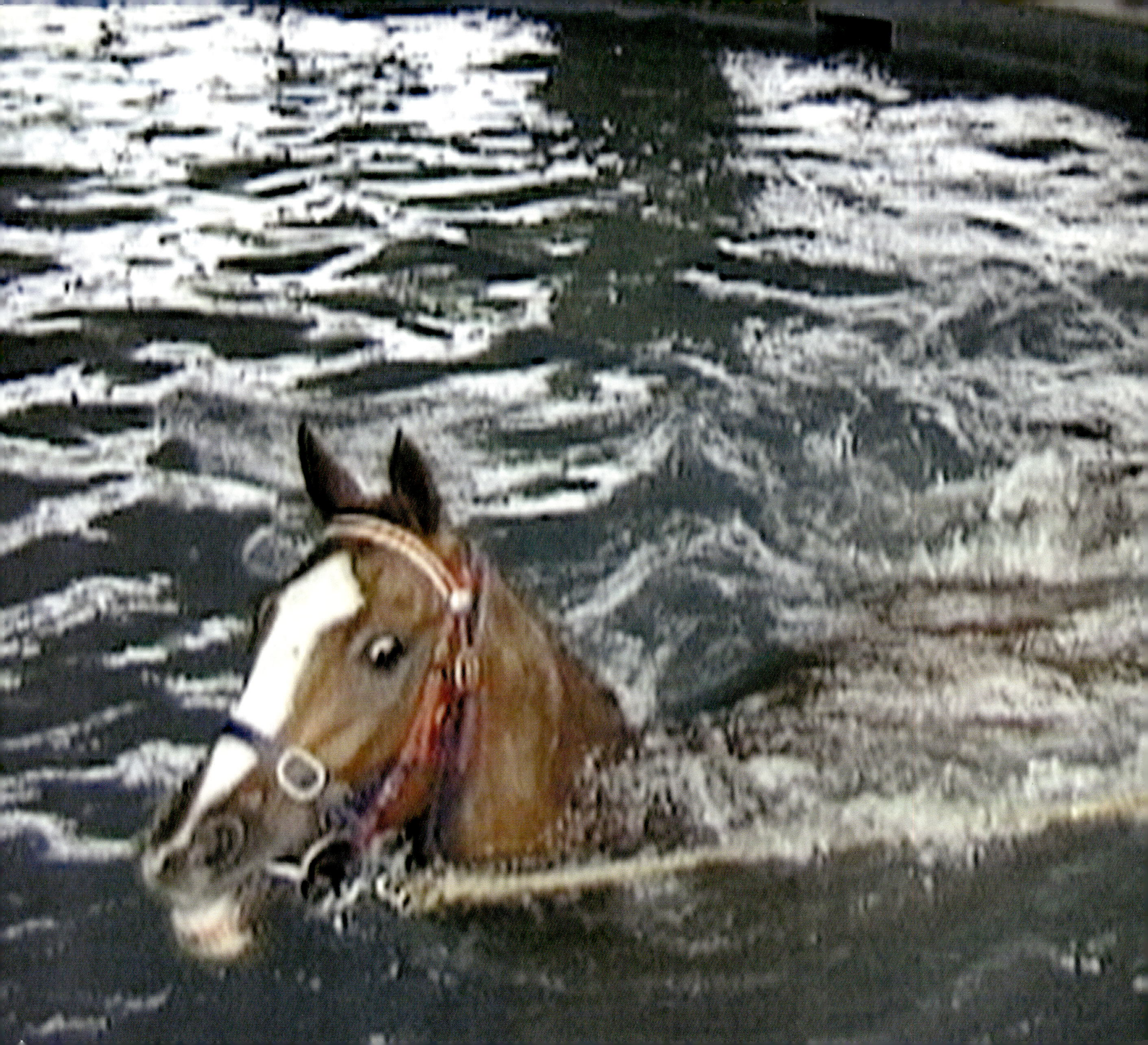

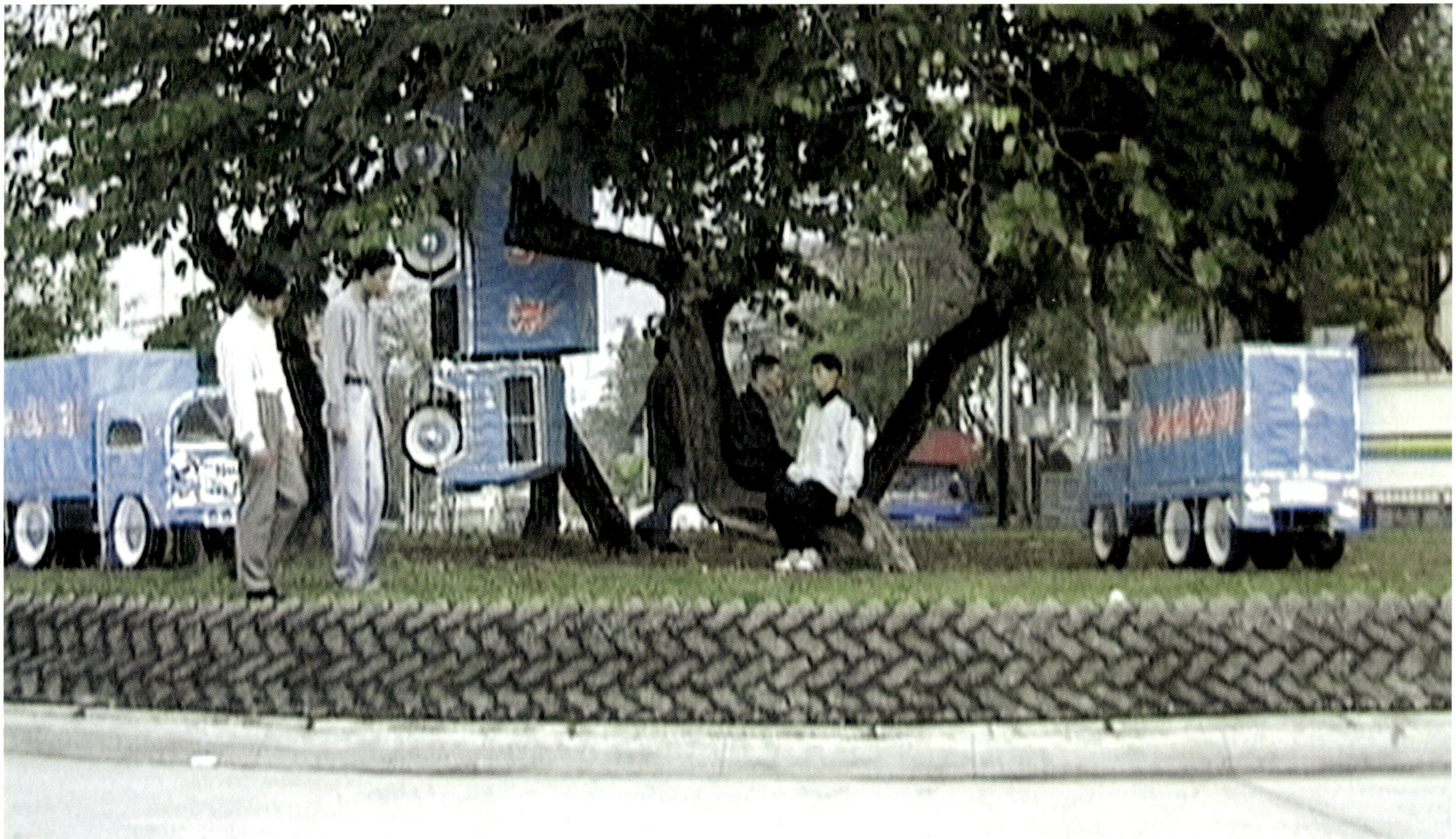

 stills from video installation **Hongkongoria**, 1997-1998

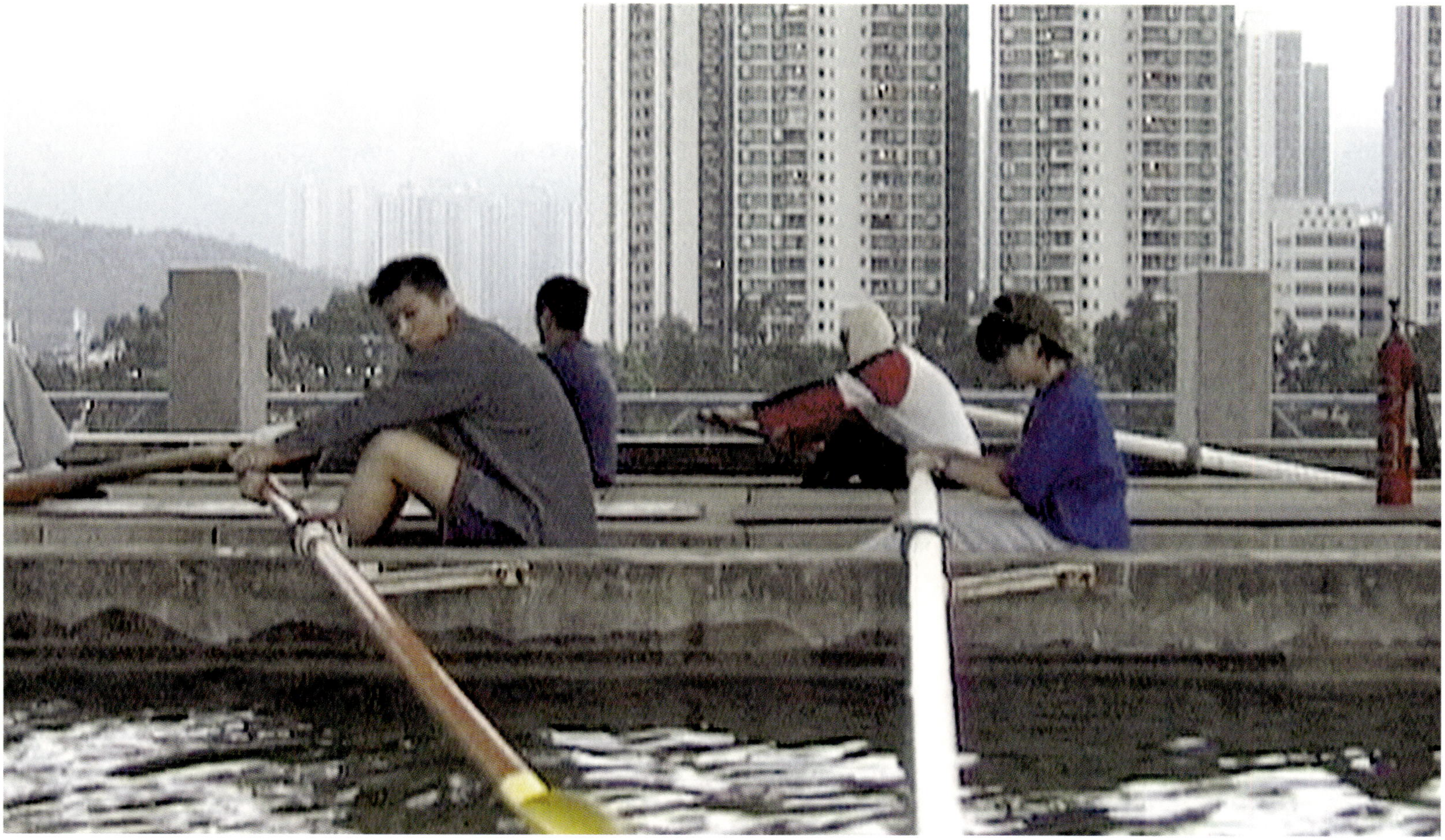

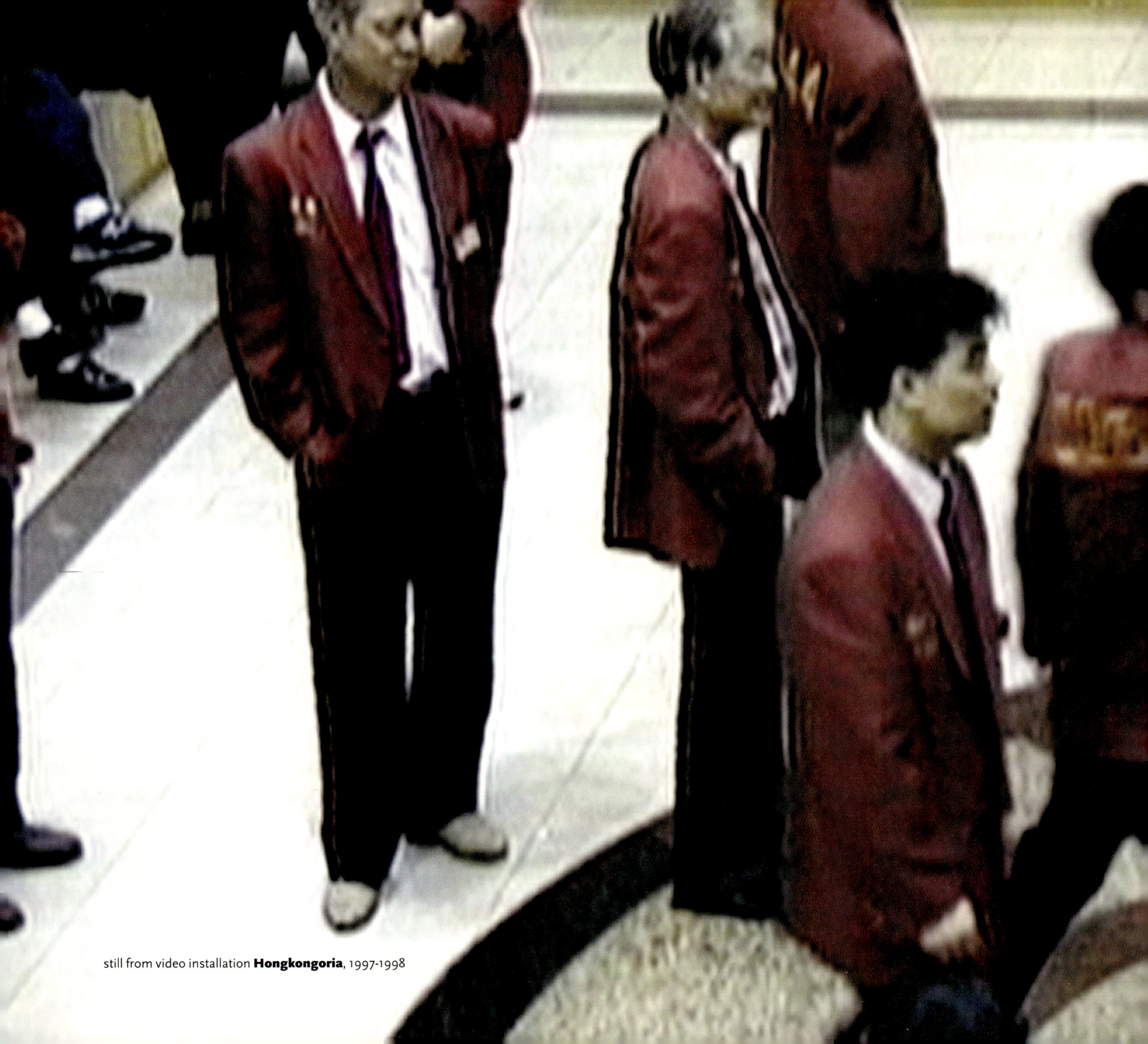

still from video installation **Hongkongoria**, 1997-1998

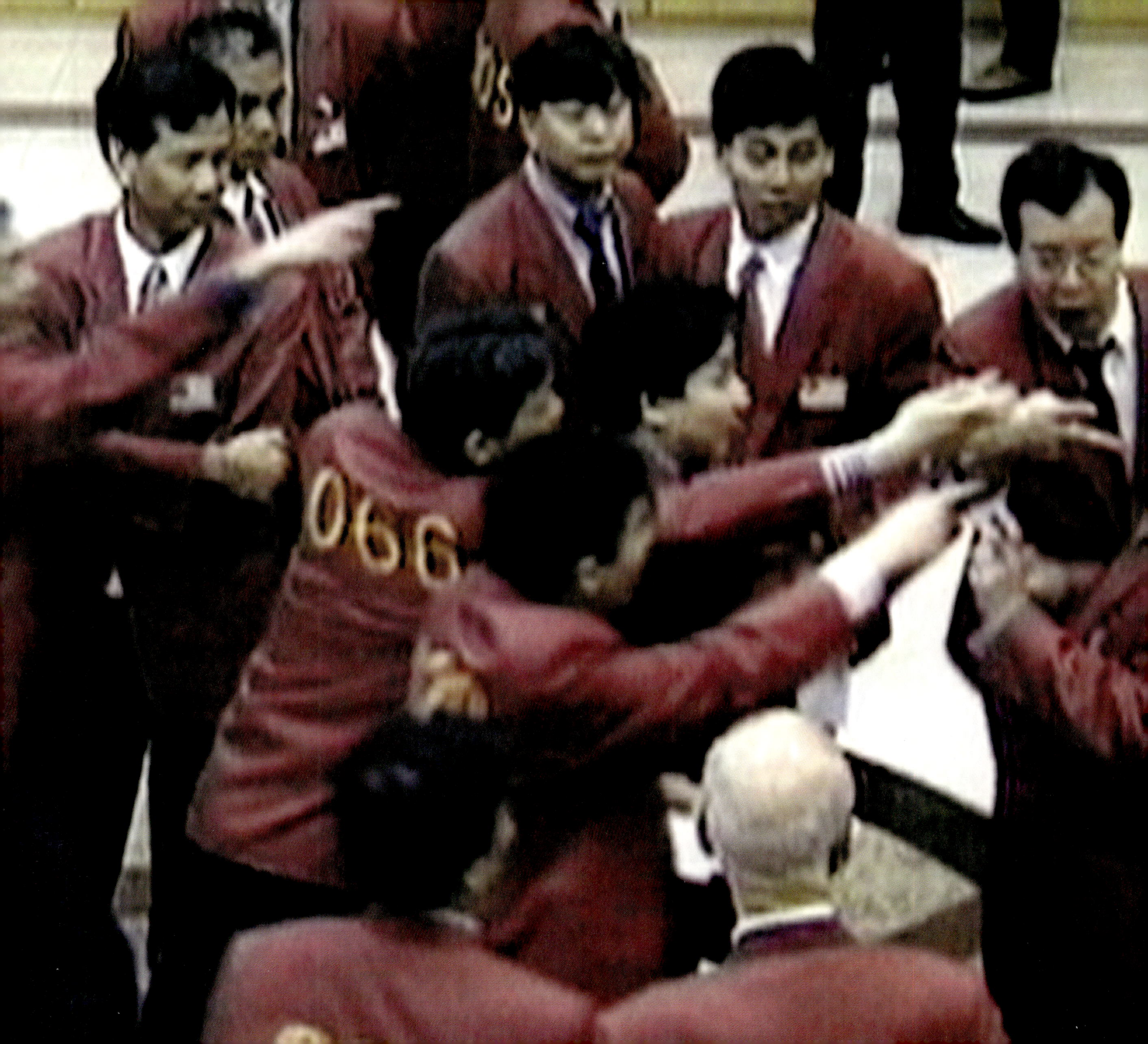
066

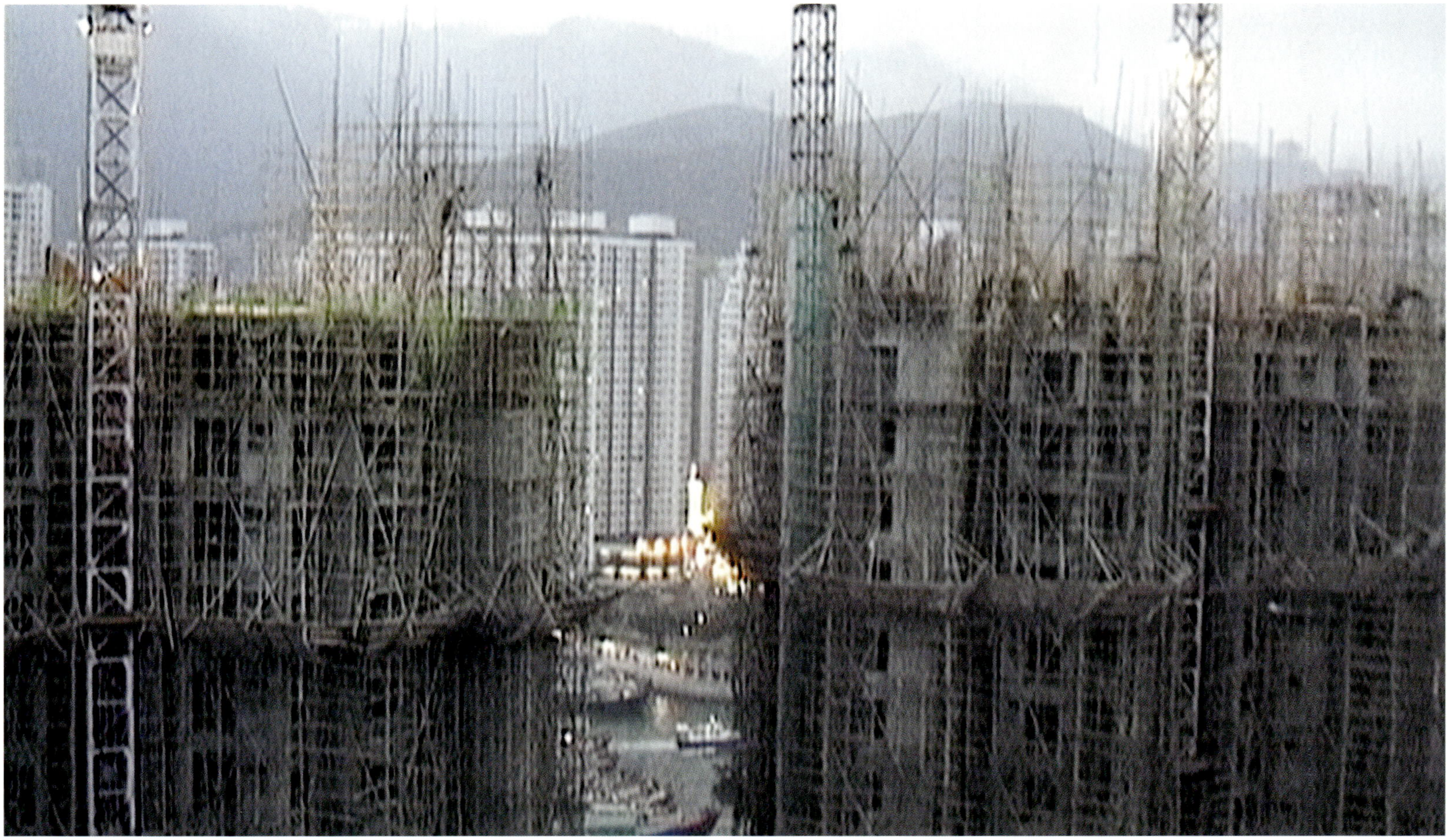

 stills from video installation **Hongkongoria**, 1997-1998

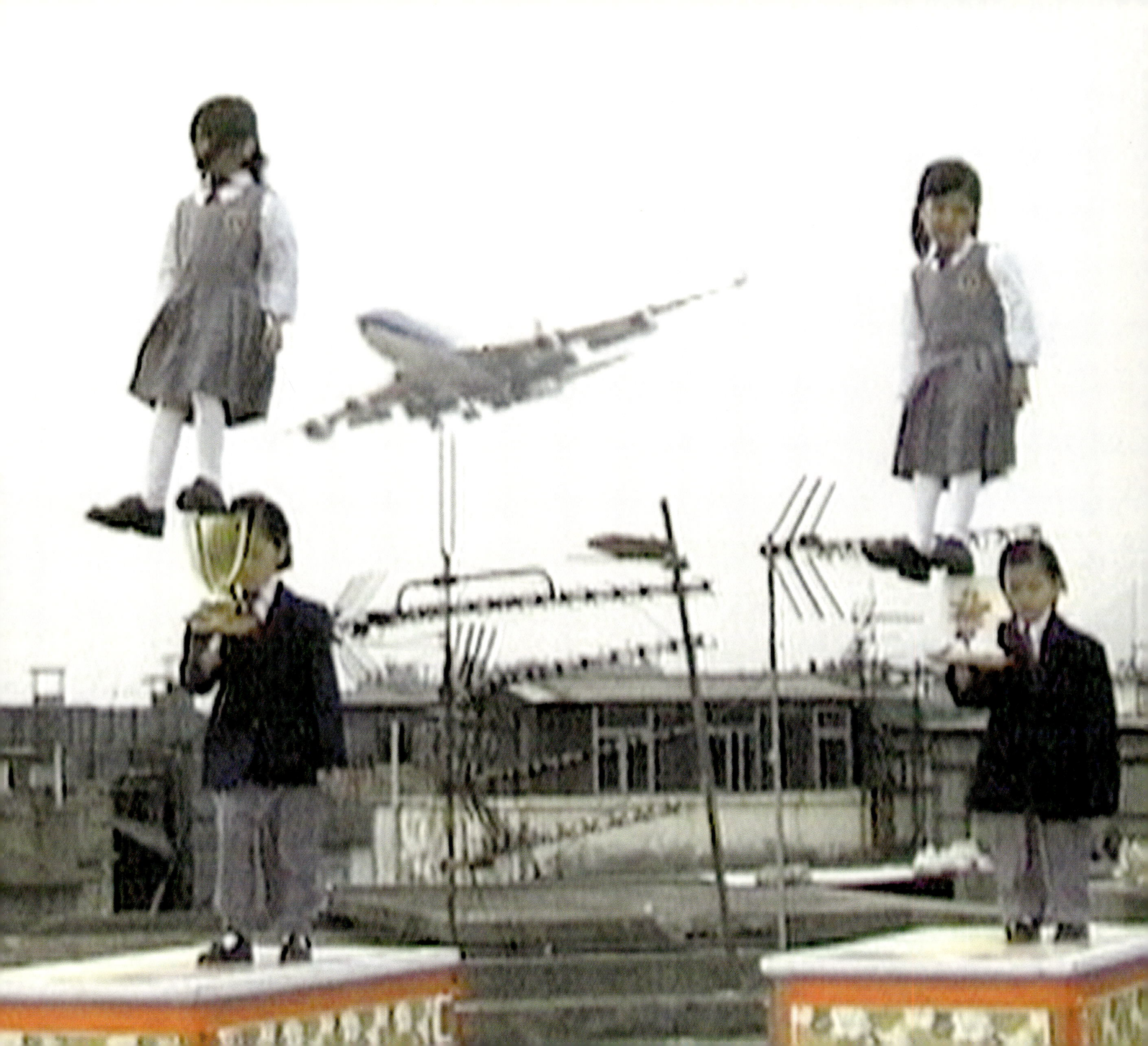

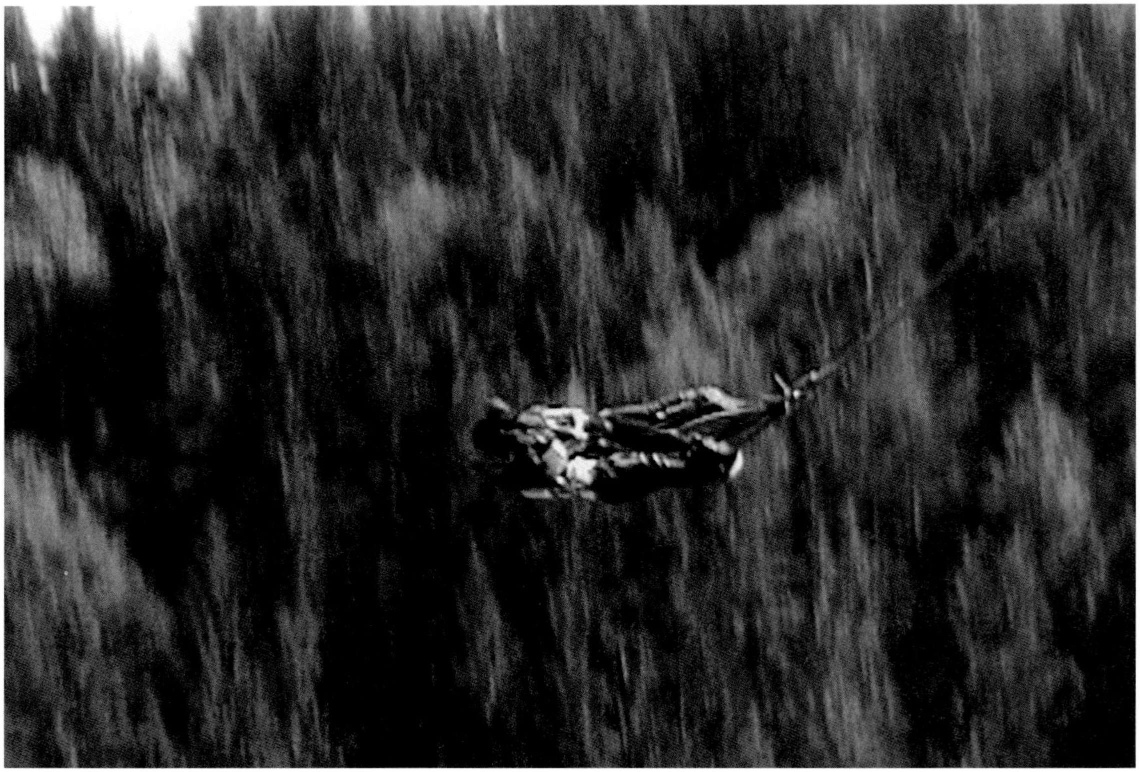

still from video installation **a small group, falling**, 1998

The Well-proportioned Cabinet

Mark Kremer

'The cabinets of gentlemen, consist in ancient medals, manuscripts, and drawings, &c. with places fitted up for some natural curiosities.'

Thomas Sheraton, *The Cabinet Dictionary* (1803)

The art of making well-proportioned cabinets has become very rare nowadays. You used to be able to find workshops all over town where cabinetmakers passed their skills on to apprentices. Now it is like looking for a needle in a haystack. Decent people who none the less know where to find a furniture workshop and how to order a cabinet, are no longer assured of a fine product.

In order to have a cabinet for his collection of rarities, K. decided to make one himself. The growth of his collection left him no choice. So many objects had been added recently that he was in danger of losing sight of the whole. A cabinet with plenty of compartments and drawers to accommodate the swollen mass would change that.

Confident that he was handy enough, K. set to work. A manual for cabinetmakers provided him with a design to his liking. He bought wood and copper and worked on the cabinet in his free hours. His parents were surprised by the sudden activity. They said nothing, but exchanged astonished glances, used as they were to a son who withdrew to his room in the evening to view his collection in peace.

Now in the evening, and sometimes at night, the sound of sawing, sanding and hammering disturbed the familiar silence. There were even times when K. came home from the insurance office where he spent his days and skipped the meal his mother had prepared because the work on the cabinet seemed more important to him. And although at first his parents were not worried by the task that K. had set himself – in the past they had often been successful in encouraging him to do odd jobs around the house – they grew alarmed when the work on the cabinet came to engross K. more and more.

One evening K. broke the silence around the progress of his enterprise. 'Father, mother', he announced solemnly, 'I have tried the patience of you both, but that will soon be over. In a few days the cabinet I have been working on for the last months will be finished and I shall be able to accommodate my collection properly. I shall show you shortly what I had in mind when I started the job.' K.'s parents were delighted with the news and proposed to celebrate the imminent opening of the cabinet with a special dinner to which they also wanted to invite one of K.'s childhood friends.

A few weeks after K.'s good news, Josef Krasinski paid a visit to the house where he and K. had played as children. It was still early on a beautiful autumn evening, the sun bathed the leaves in a golden yellow glow; nature was waning. Josef Krasinski was a representative of an international trading company. He often travelled on business. He had grown up in K.'s small town but had left it as soon as he could. By now his experiences in remote cities and countries had made him a man of the world. The consequent level of cultivation was expressed in his case in a wide and refined repertoire of formalities that had become second nature to his public performance.

With his hat in his left hand, Josef Krasinski stood before the house of K.'s parents on this autumn evening. He reached for the door-knocker with his free hand. Three times a metallic sound rang out. Muffled noises could be heard in the distance, and as he waited for the door to open he let his mind wander a last time to the letter addressed to him in which tonight's event had been announced without any further explanation. Was it wise to respond to an invitation from someone he had not had any contact with for a long time? His curiosity had brought him here, but what if the intention was not well meant? It would not be the first time that others had tried to enlist his services because of his good connections.

He stopped musing when the door opened and K.'s parents welcomed him. 'Welcome, Josef Krasinski! Thank you for coming. Our son will be delighted to see his old childhood friend again. It is very good that you are here. The creation that he is going to present this evening will now be seen by someone who has seen a lot of the world. It will be fascinating to hear your response.'

K.'s parents spoke in turn, respectfully but rather awkwardly, as if they did not really know who they had in front of them: the slight young man of the past whose appearance was stored in their memory, or the impressive figure who stood before them. Josef Krasinski put them at ease with a few delicately chosen remarks. Then they led their guest through a long, dark hall leading to the dining room. At the end, Josef Krasinski saw the silhouette of K., who approached him after the first formalities were over. Josef Krasinski immediately recognised the bony, barely altered features of his old friend. He walked towards him and bowed gracefully.

The arrival of Josef Krasinski had no discernible effect on K.. His welcome was a stiff greeting. He accompanied his guest to the dining room, showed him to his place, and sat down. K.'s mother served a three-course dinner. The company ate with relish, and Josef Krasinski complimented K.'s mother several times. He also made entertaining conversation on his work as a representative and his experiences during the past years. K. did not take up his cautious attempts to open the subject of what was to happen this evening, though his manner was pleasant enough.

In the meantime K. sized up his guest. He examined his suave features intensely, as if to gauge whether the smooth skin might reveal signs that were less attuned to the laws of courtesy. K. concluded his observations when the coffee was served. While the cups were still being filled he

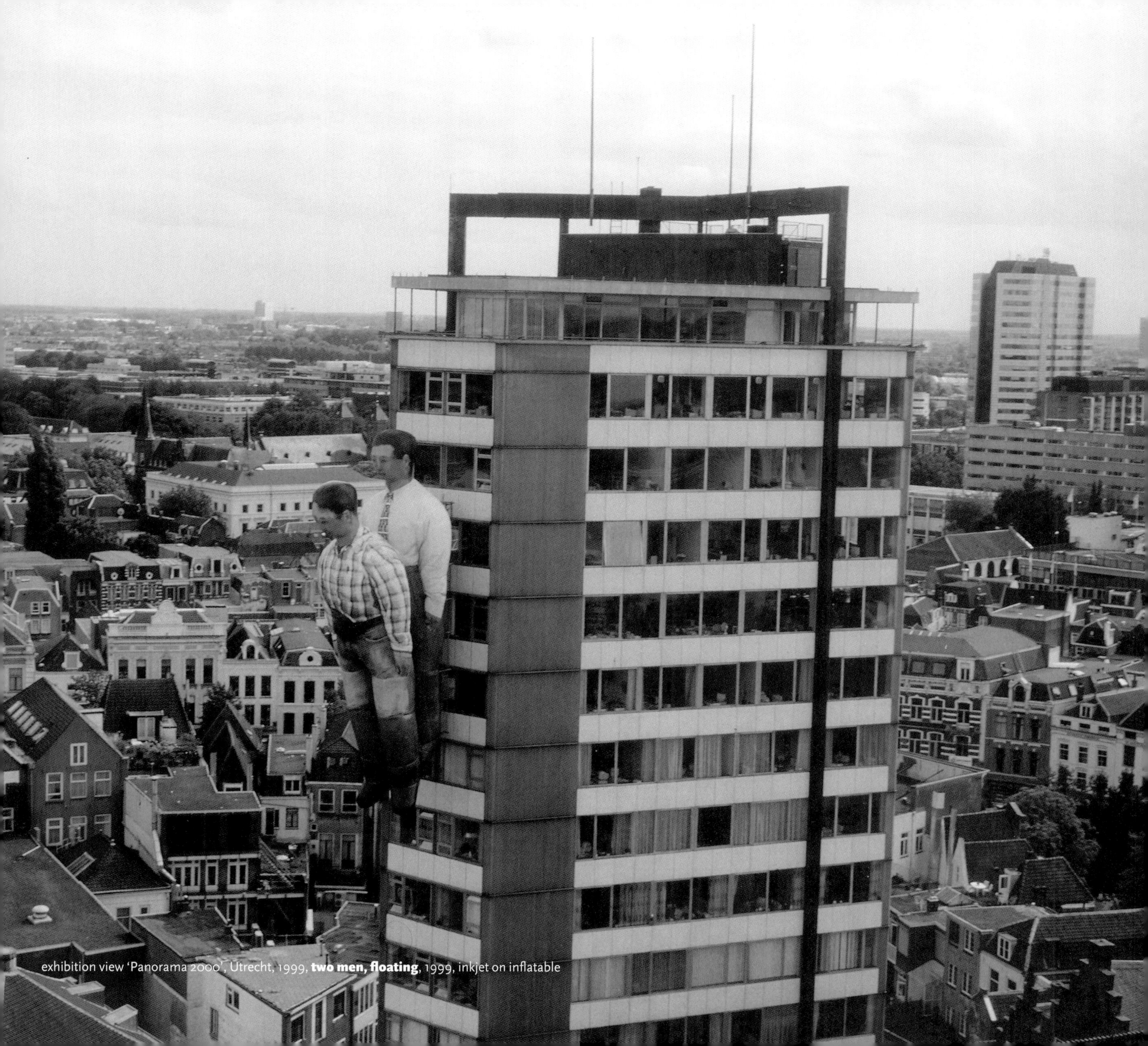

exhibition view 'Panorama 2000', Utrecht, 1999, **two men, floating**, 1999, inkjet on inflatable stood up and asked the company to follow him to the room in which he was to present his creation. K. had hung a curtain in front of his cabinet. After a brief introduction dealing mainly with the technical nature of his activities over the last months, he pulled the curtain to one side. What was revealed was a cabinet, manufactured in the finest mahogany and decorated with ornamental copperwork. The cabinet contained some twenty compartments and drawers that were almost all filled with objects from K.'s collection. One by one, K. took the objects in his hand. Most of them were groups of figures that appeared exotic due to the colours and materials used. For instance, there were opium-smokers in porcelain, and a pendant with the same figures engaged in stylised combat. There were also figures of dreamers, figures in the grip of the most powerful emotions, and people who threw themselves into a ravine for no apparent reason.

K. commented incisively on each object. He mentioned the maker, explained what the object represented, and how it had come into his collection. He spoke without stopping, barely paying any heed to his audience. At the end of his speech he set the objects back in the cabinet, sat down and looked at his guest, awaiting his reaction.

K.'s parents had stood aloof all this time. Apparently they were familiar with their son's story. Their attention was focused on Josef Krasinski. It was as if they had emptied themselves, so that K.'s words could penetrate the body of his guest directly without encountering the slightest resistance from anyone else in the room.

In this, they were totally successful. During K.'s speech Josef Krasinski had paid no heed to his surroundings, his attention riveted on the objects commented on by K.. He was taken aback. The world that K. conjured up for him in this room seemed strange, but then again not. In his mind he ran through a film of his past experiences. Meetings with people on some business matter took on a different aspect when he tried to see them in the light of the human activity that K. talked about. He had come across all sorts of figures, in bars and offices, in restaurants and hotel lobbies. But had he got to know them? No, he was bound to reply, and anyway how could he know people whose behaviour was completely dictated by business? Time and again he had been confronted by a stranger, whose outward appearance might well have masked someone who longed for something entirely different in life.

Josef Krasinski fell into a great sadness. He realised that he was not very different from the people in his thoughts. He had remained a stranger to himself, a man whose impeccable self-presentation was a facade behind which lurked someone who really wanted to dream, to fight or have fun, like the figures in K.'s collection. If only it were that simple. This evening his inner life was less clear to him than ever.

Somehow or other Josef Krasinski thanked K. for his talk. This evening, he said, he had heard things which would gladden him for a long time. K.'s story about his collection had made such an impression that it was difficult for him to show his appreciation properly. But he hoped that there would soon be an opportunity to discuss it further with K. After expressing his gratitude to K.'s parents for their warm hospitality, Josef Krasinski left the house of his childhood friend. Those remaining in the house saw him slowly walk down the street on the way to a hotel on the edge of K.'s small town.

That night Josef Krasinski dreamed about K.'s cabinet. In his dream the cabinet stood in a square in the town, and it had grown into a building with several floors. The rooms contained groups of people who were enjoying themselves in ways that were sometimes not easy for an outsider to make out. Josef Krasinski walked through the corridors of the building. Determined to join one of the groups, he looked through the lighted windows of the rooms. Everywhere he was denied access, and where he was admitted it was only to be ignored. At his wits' end, he sat down on a chair in a corridor. He rested his head in his hands, and was overwhelmed by a sense of defeat.

Just when he was about to give up entirely because he was not welcome anywhere, he saw K., who understood the situation immediately. K. took a key out of his pocket. 'This key opens a room in this building that is for you alone', K. said. 'There you can be yourself.' He explained how Josef Krasinski was to reach it. Overjoyed, Josef Krasinski set out for the room K. had indicated, opened the door, and walked into a room where a group of men and women dressed as cowboys and indians were playing what looked like a cruel game. The welcome he received was not exactly encouraging. They rushed towards him with knives, axes and pistols. He felt as if his last hour had arrived.

At that moment Josef Krasinski awoke. He wanted to say 'It was only a dream', but for some reason he could not find his voice. It was as if someone else had taken control, someone or something that directed his movements from the outside. He had no will of his own. An invisible force now drove him out of his bed and made it clear that he must return to the place where he had spent the previous evening. He managed to dress himself properly and moved his body mechanically towards the house of K.'s parents. When they opened the door to him, he rushed past them, raced through the hall towards K.'s room and dropped down in front of the cabinet. Just before, he took up the pose of someone who has fired a shot into the air and knows that he has missed the target.

Project for Conference Center La Vie, 1993, live installation at Festival aan de Werf, Utrecht, 1993

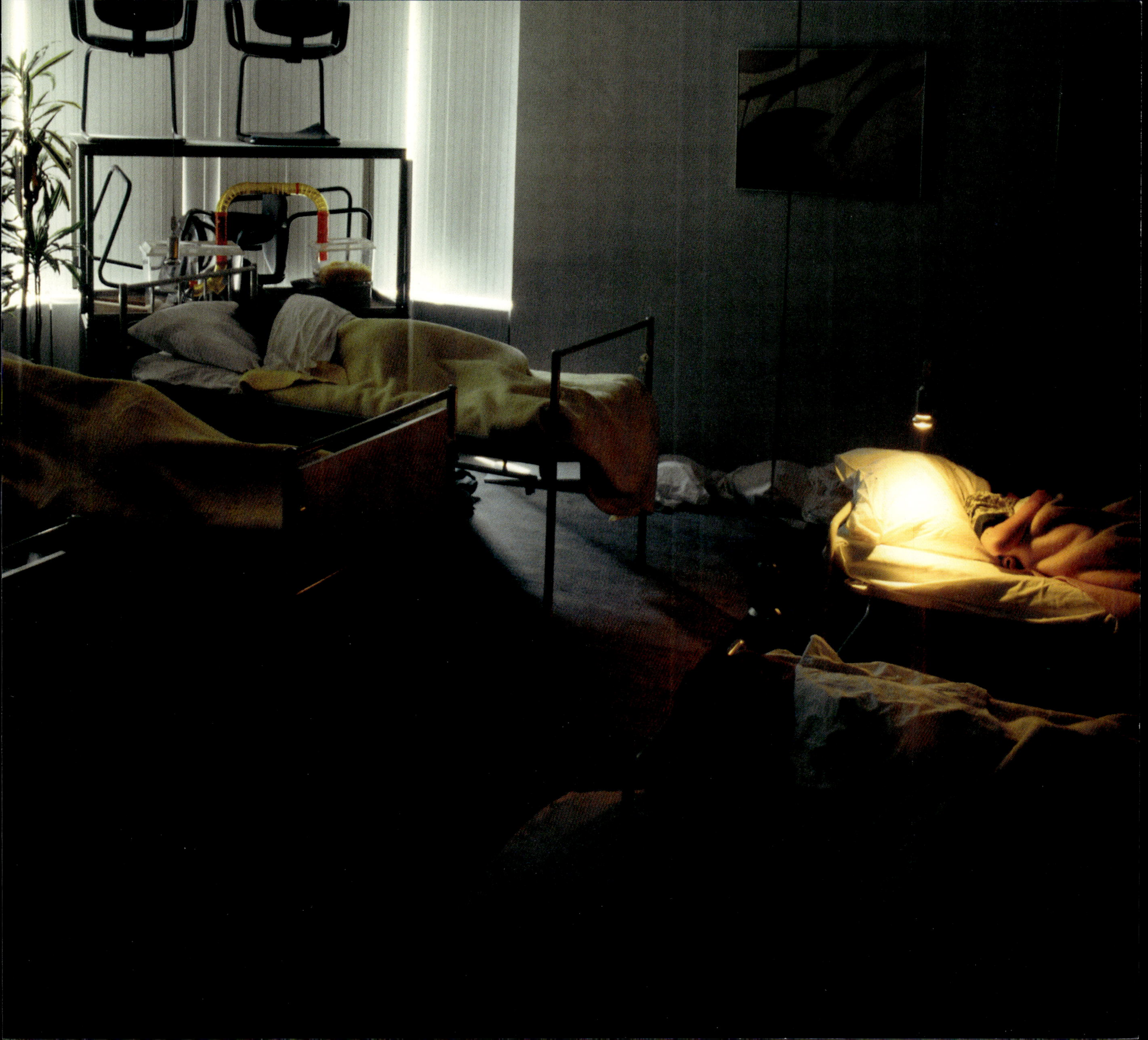

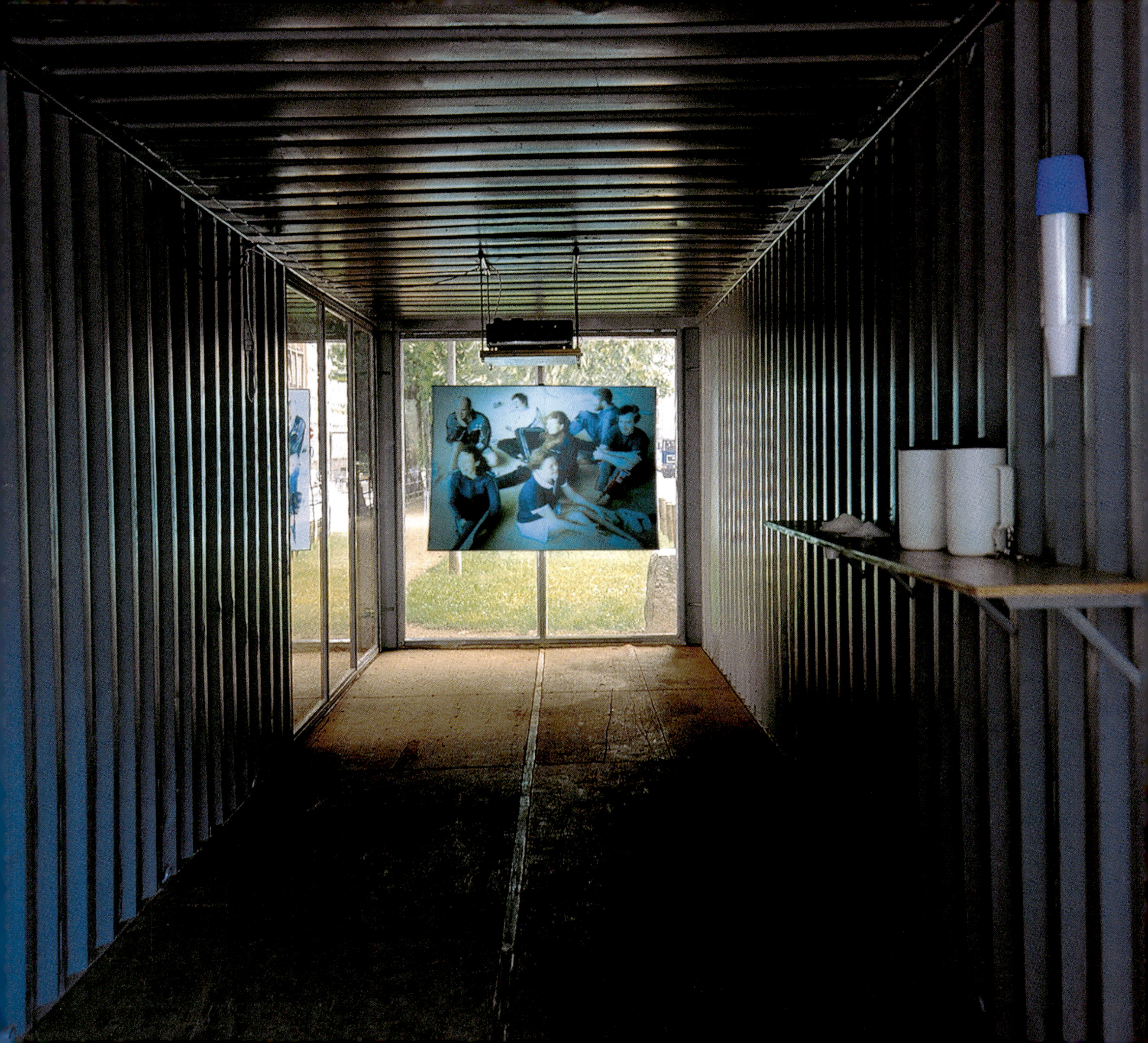

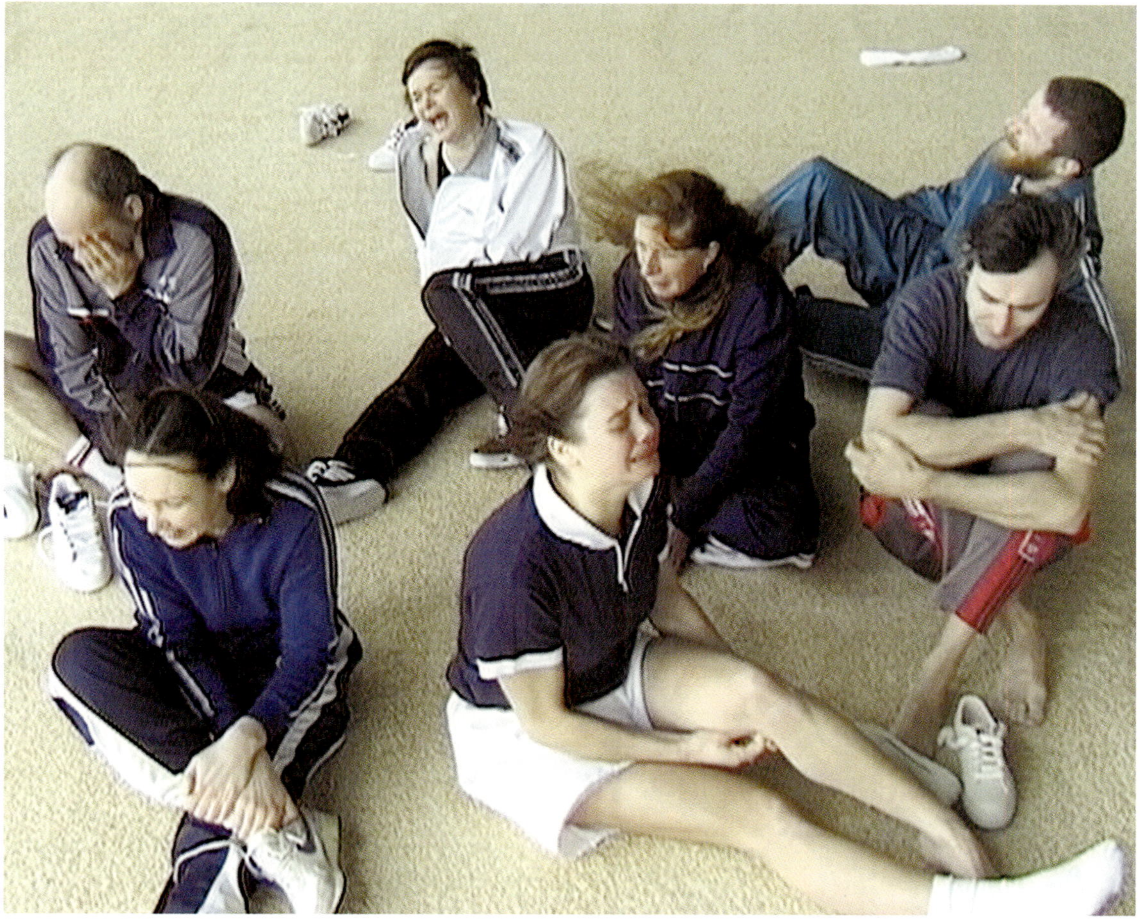

exhibition view 'Do All Oceans Have Walls', Bremen, 1998, mixed media installation and still from video installation **3 laughing and 4 crying**, 1998 exhibition view 'Hanging around', Museum Ludwig, Cologne, 1999, **Territorium**, 1999, 2 screen video installation

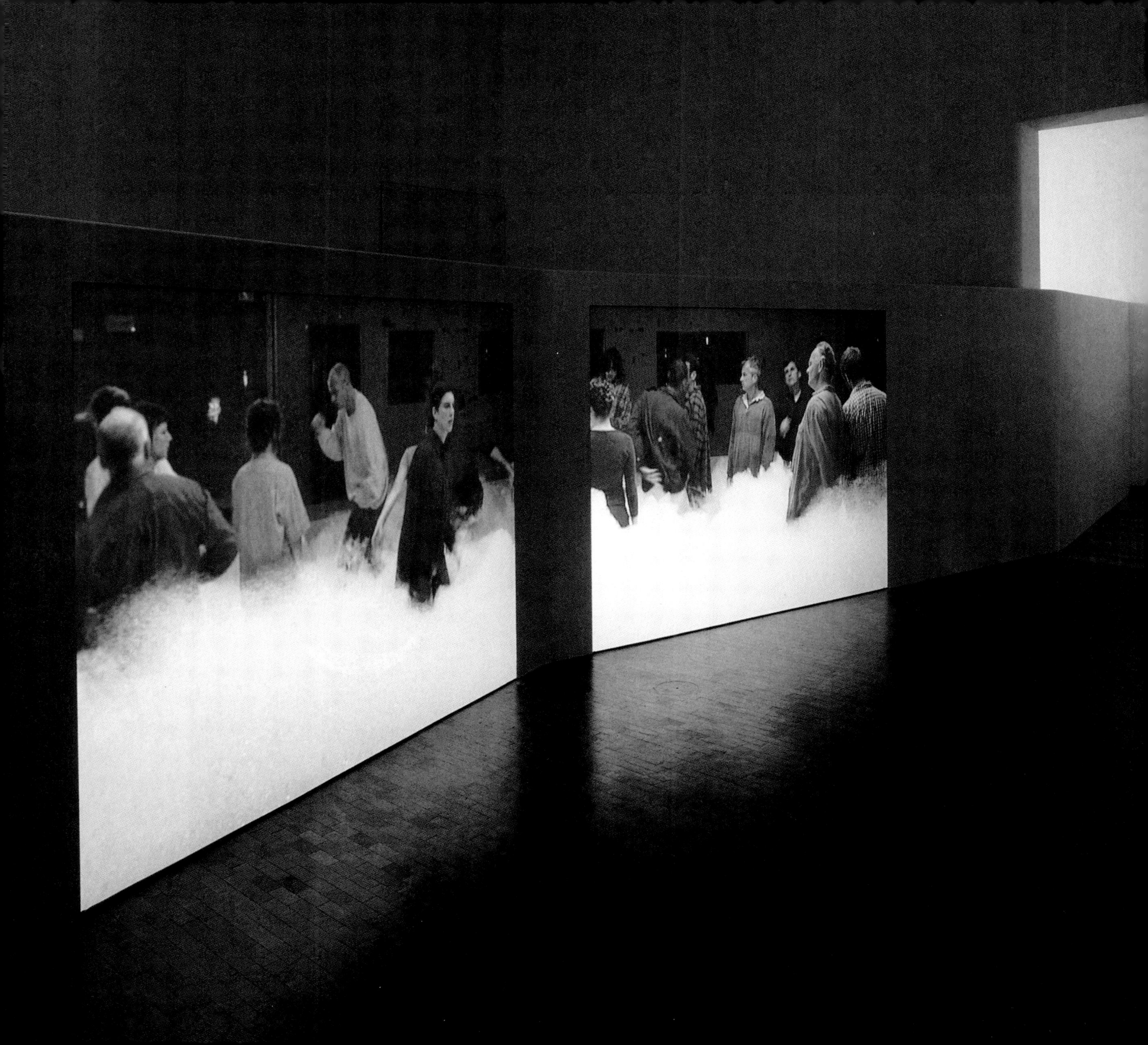

stills from video installation **Territorium**, 1999

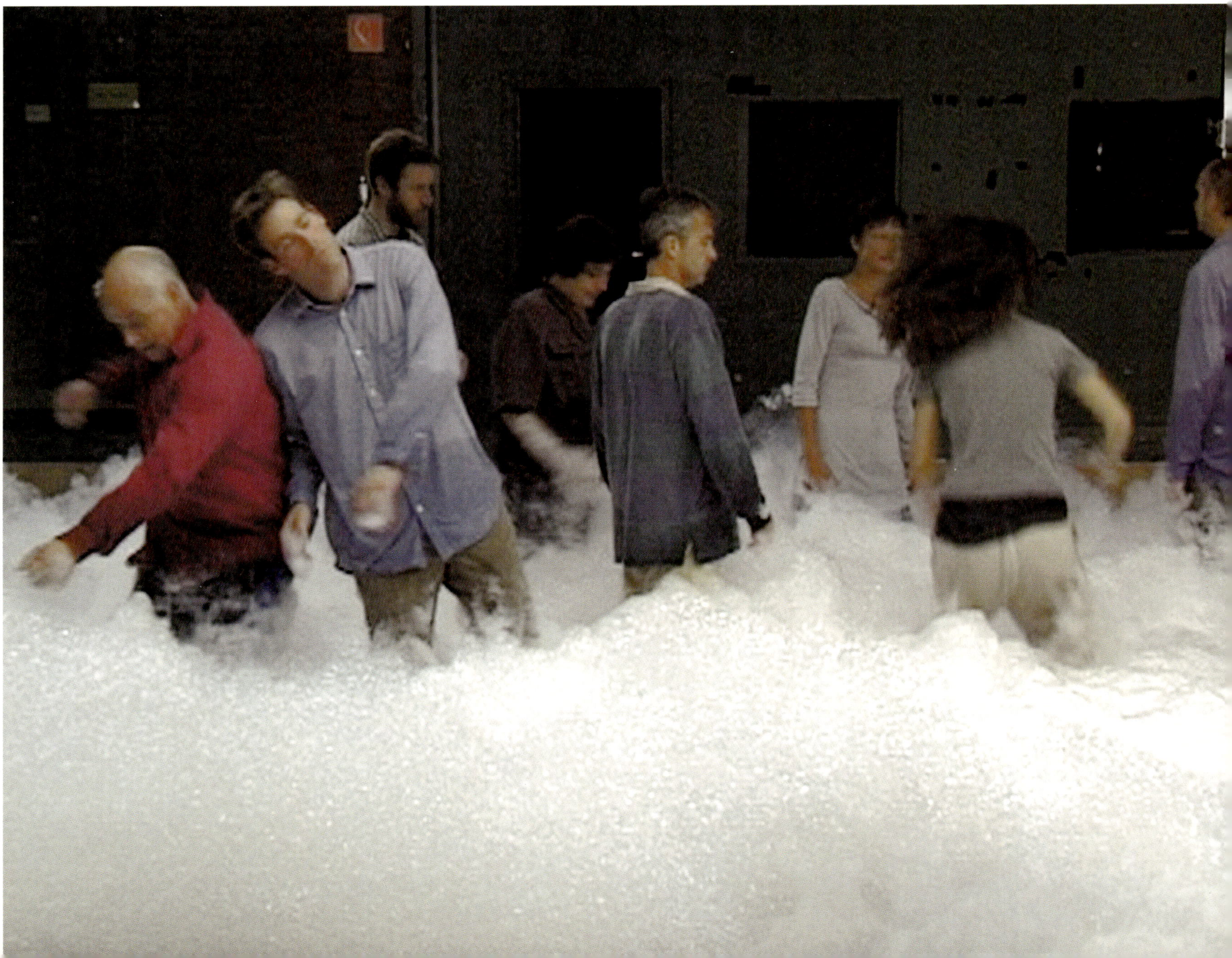

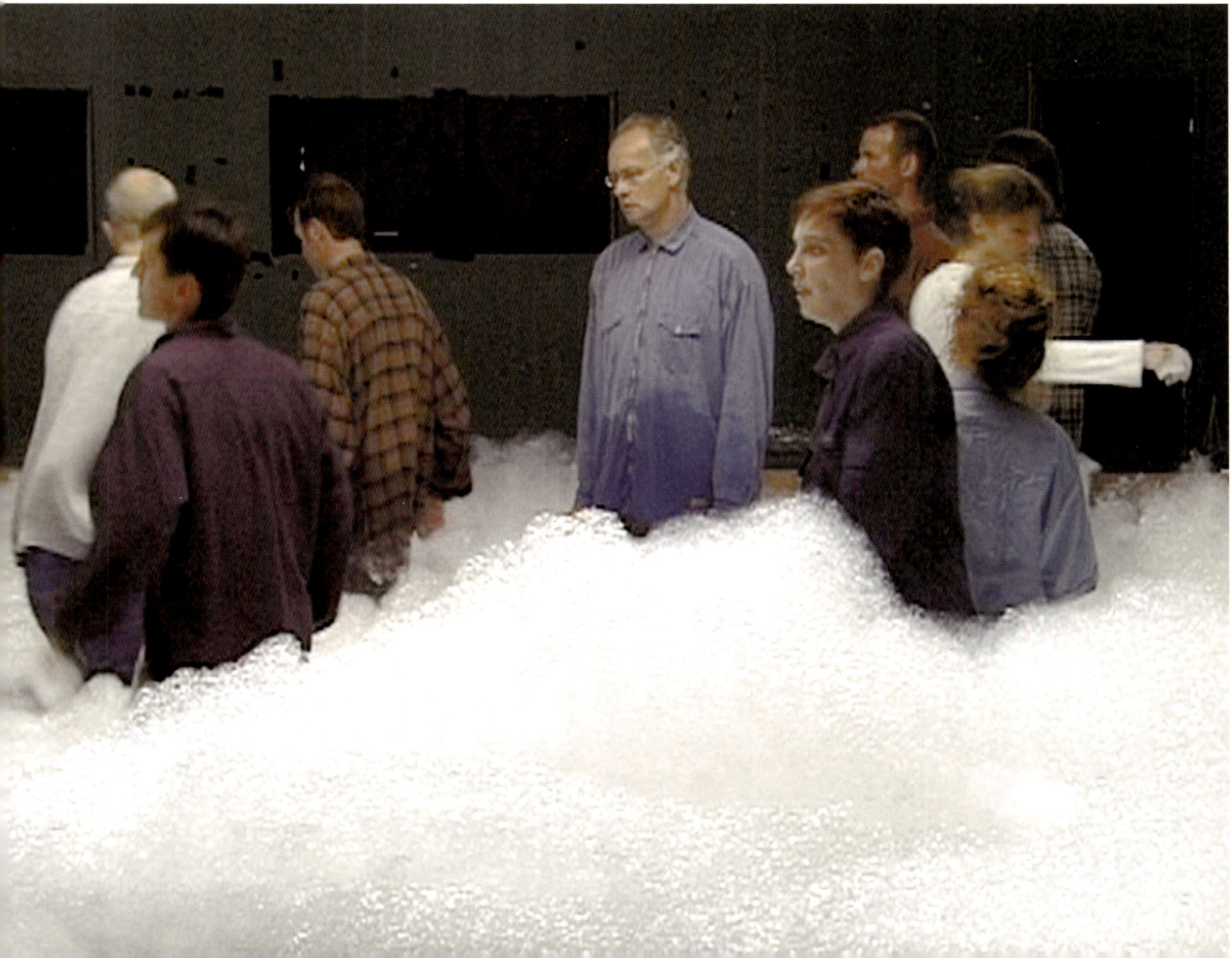

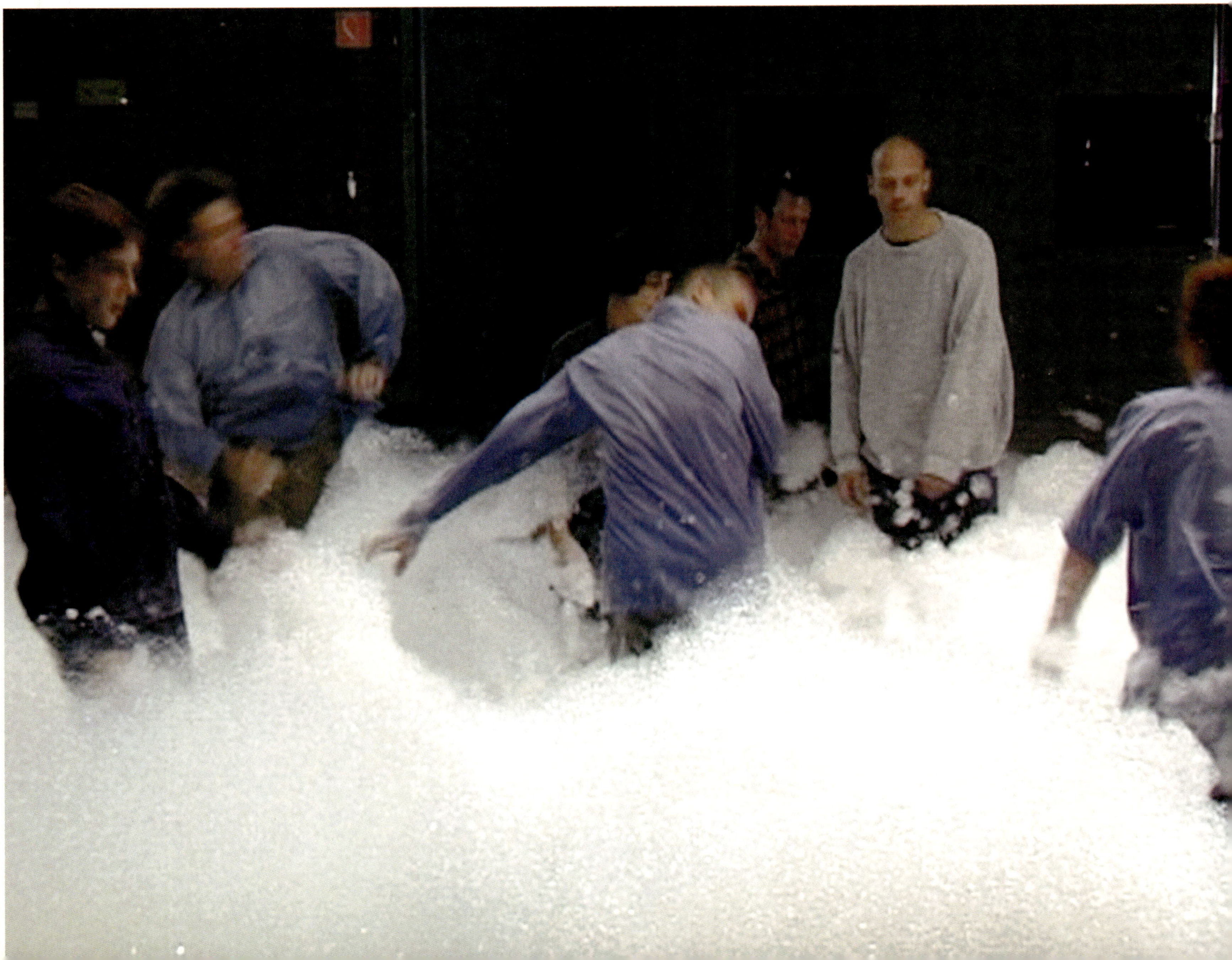

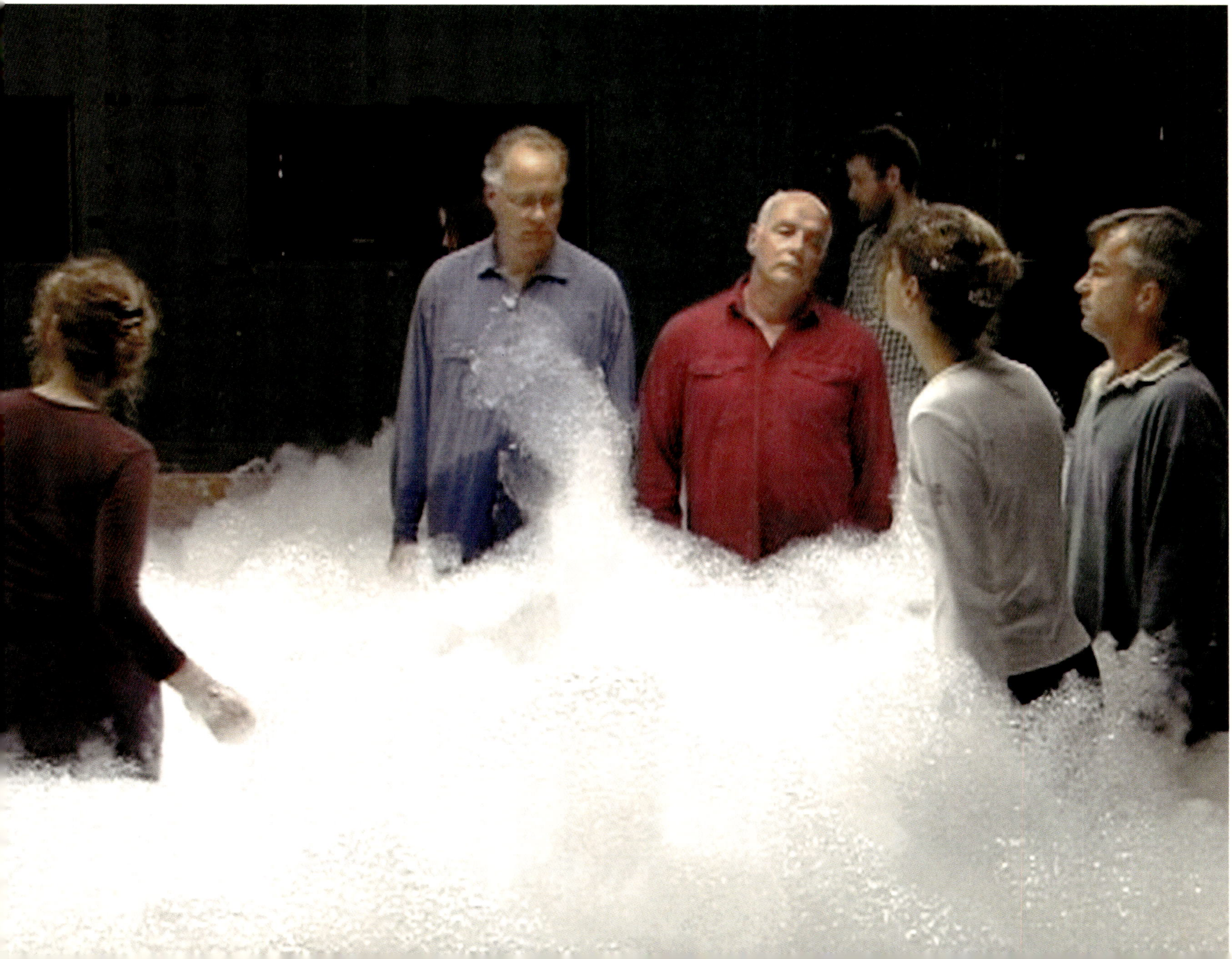

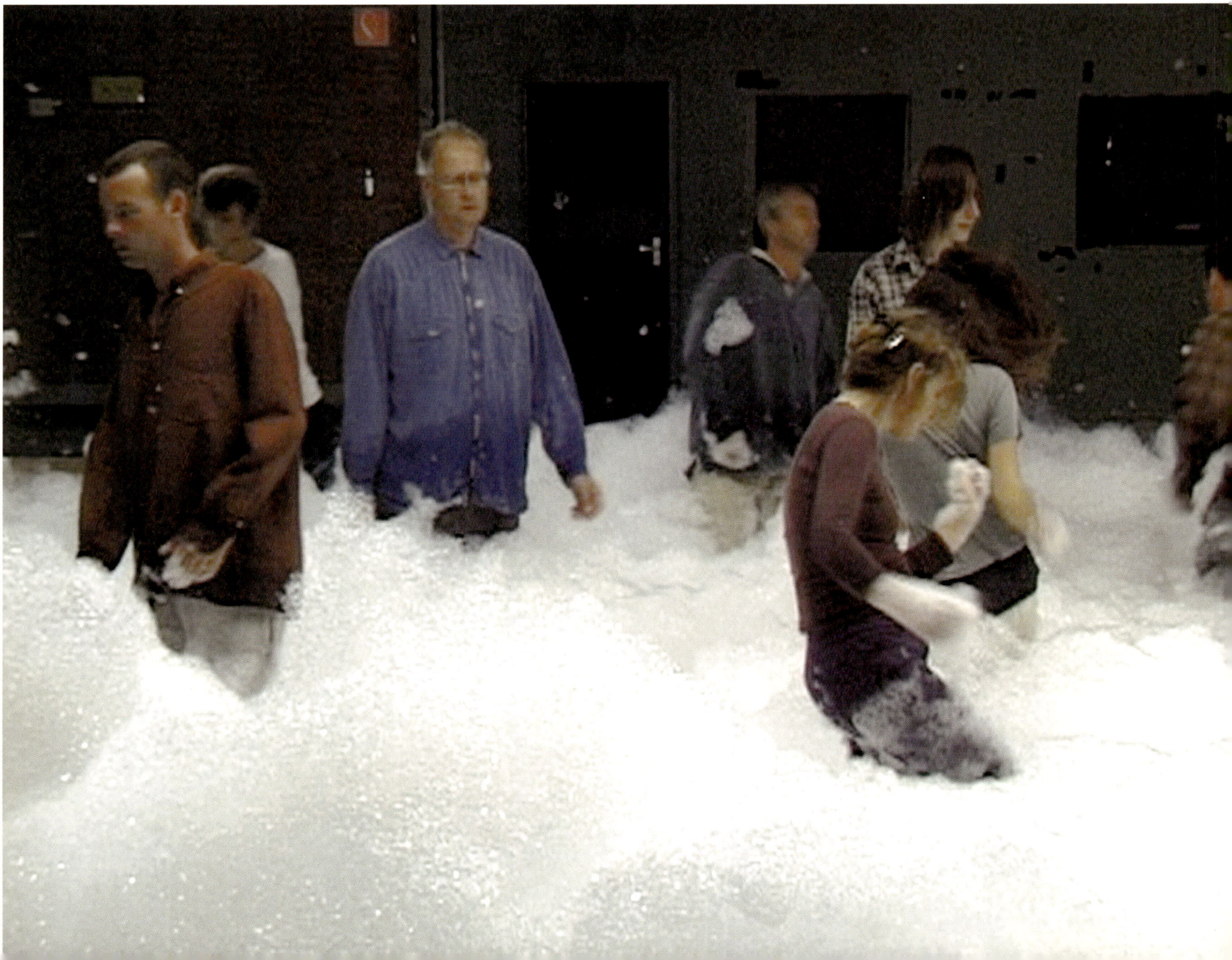

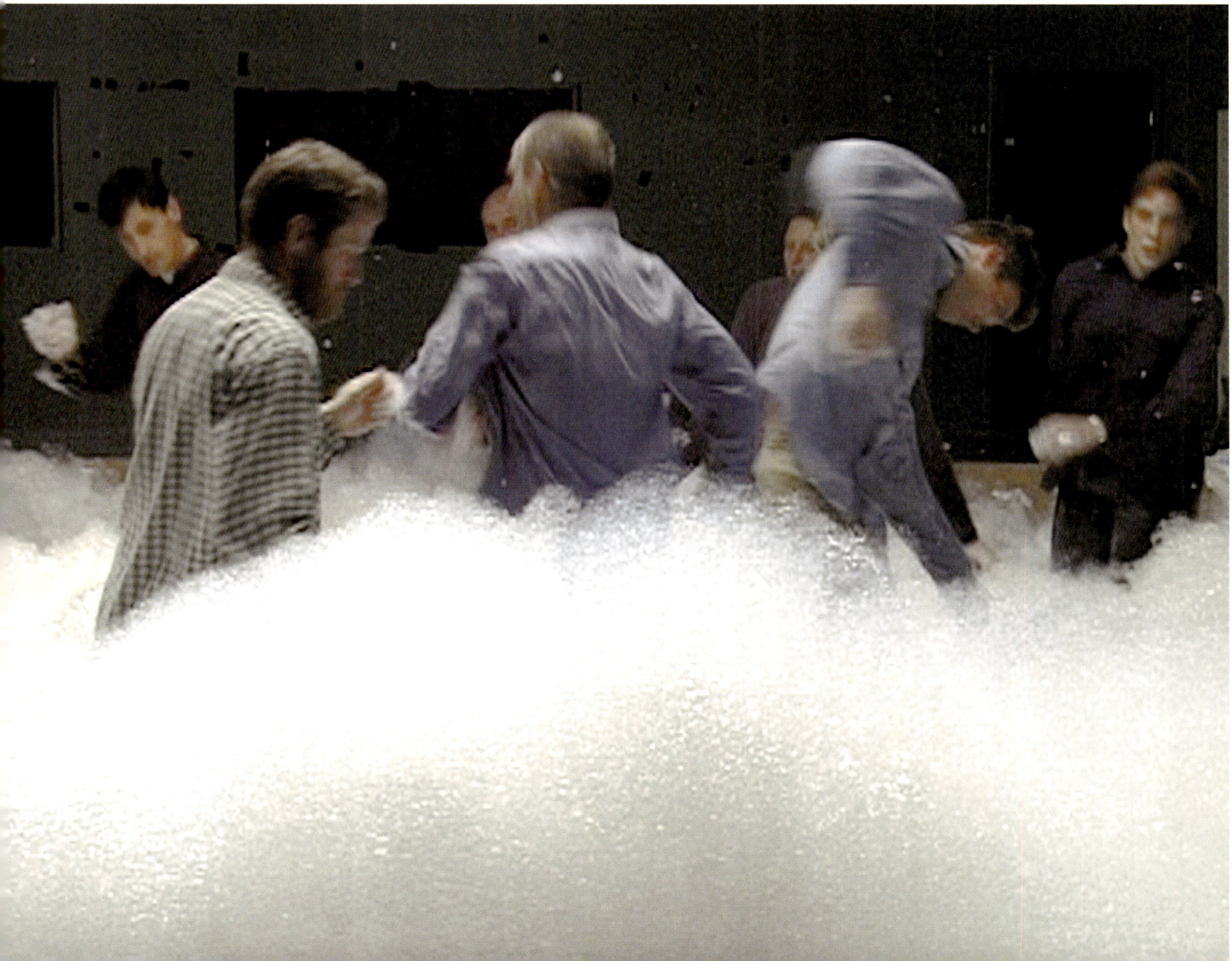

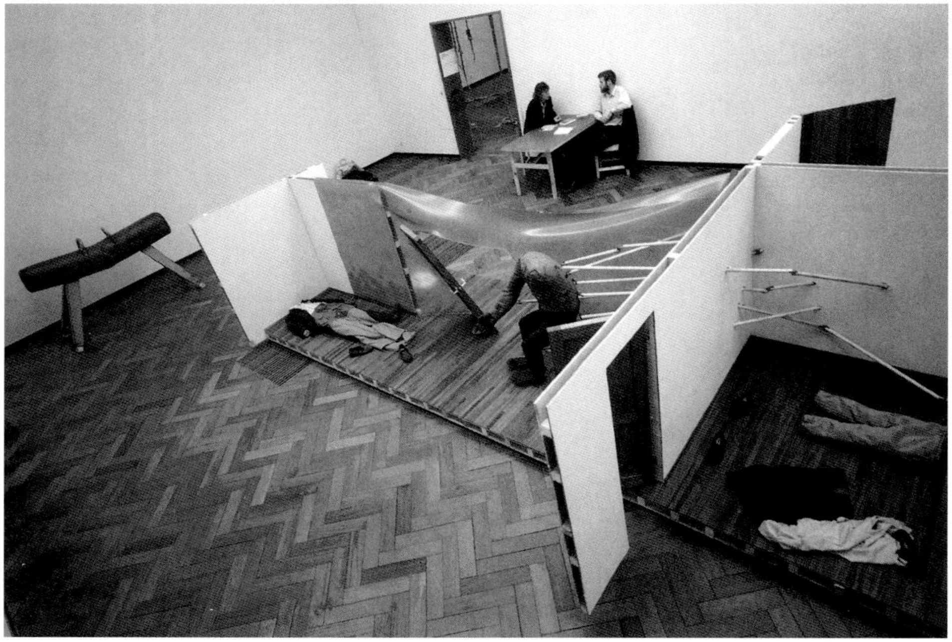

 Blue Sinkhole, 1995, live installation at the exhibition 'Wild Walls', Stedelijk Museum, Amsterdam, 1995

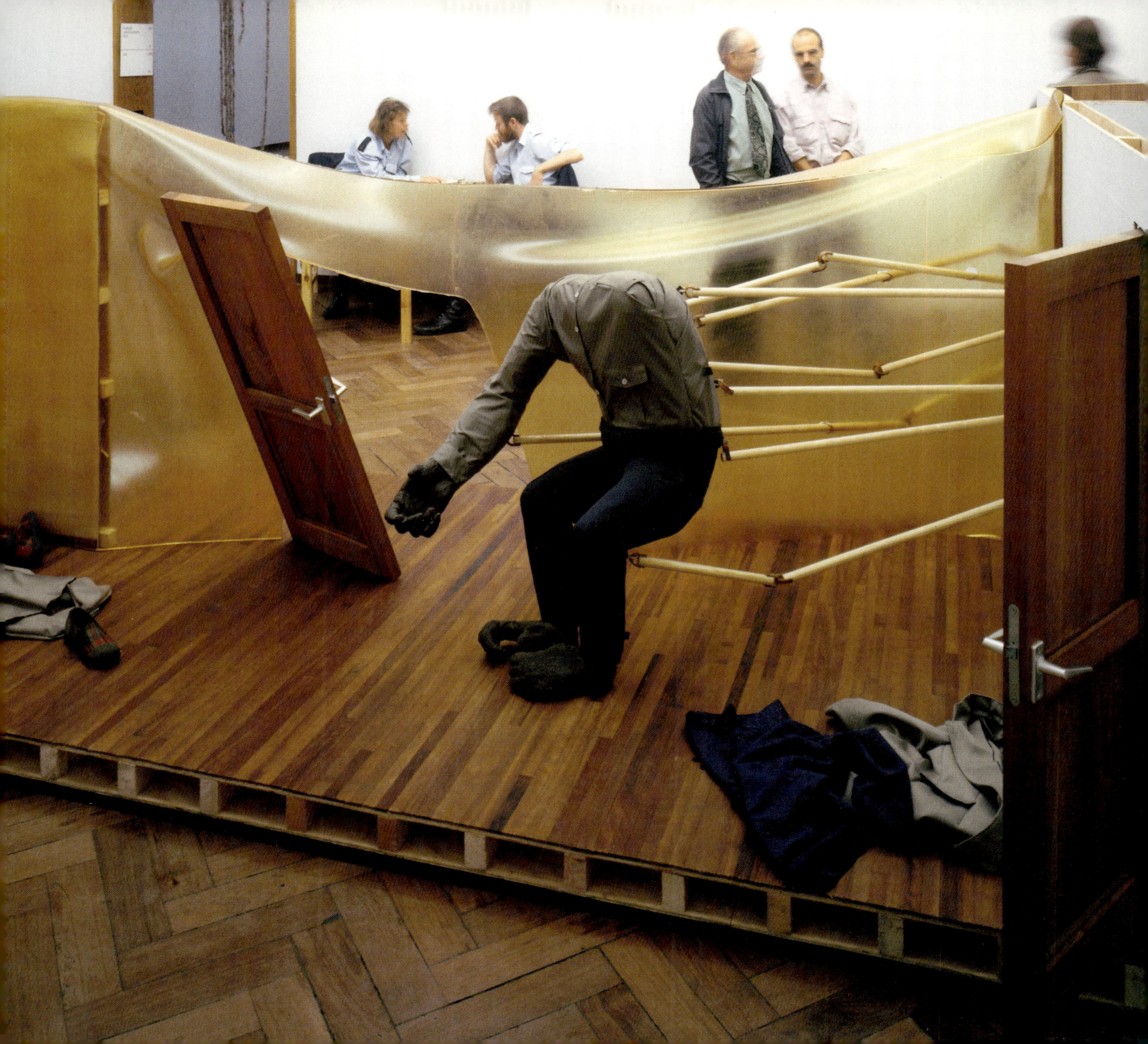

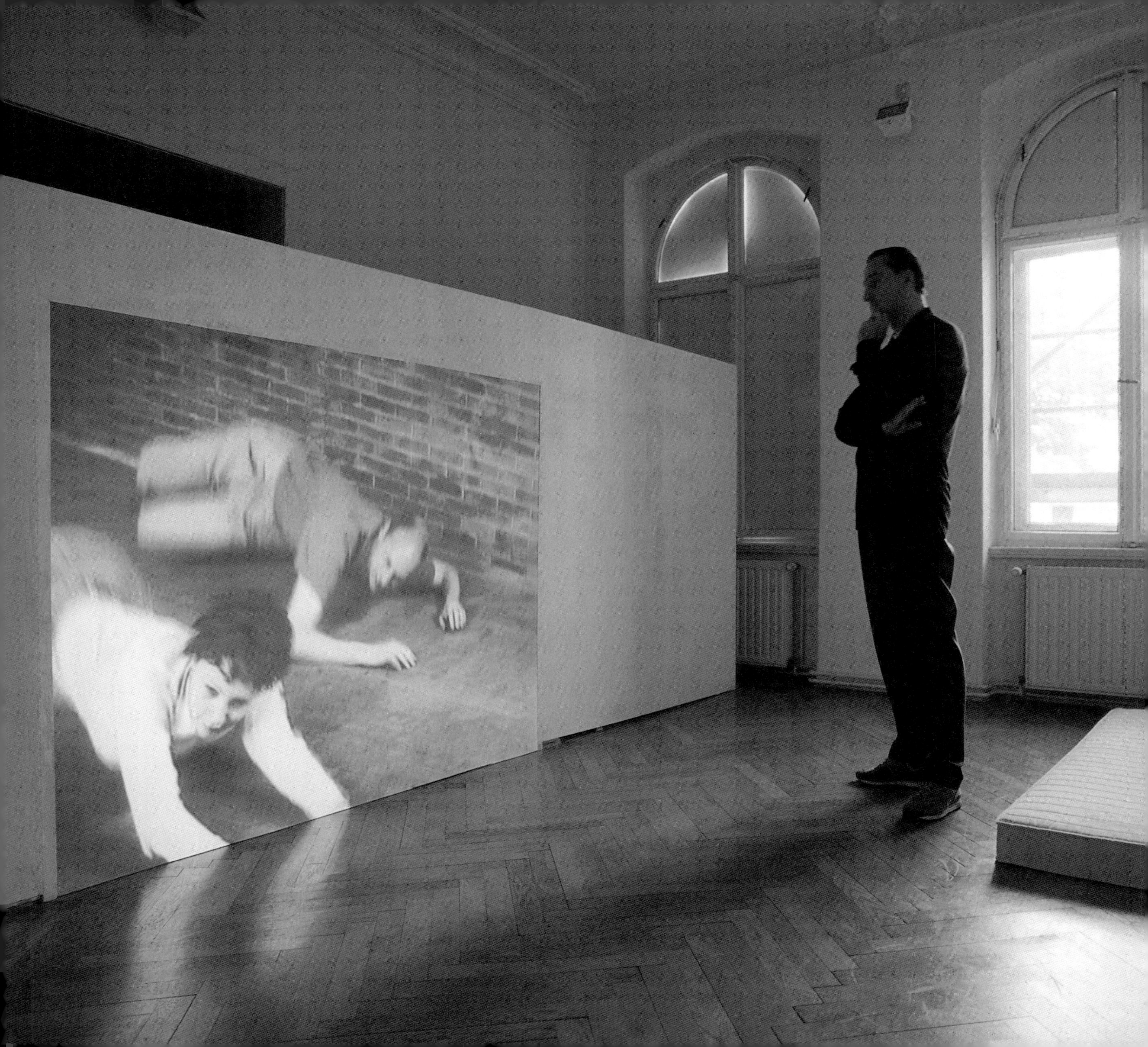

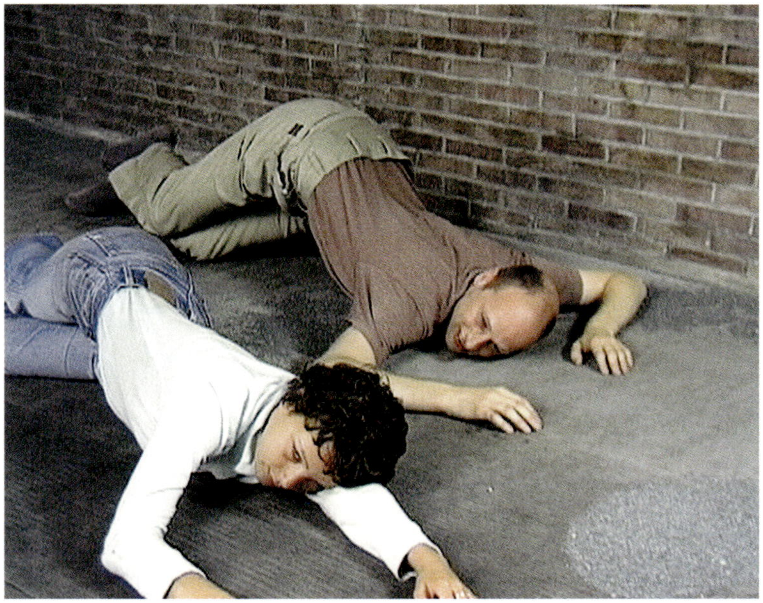

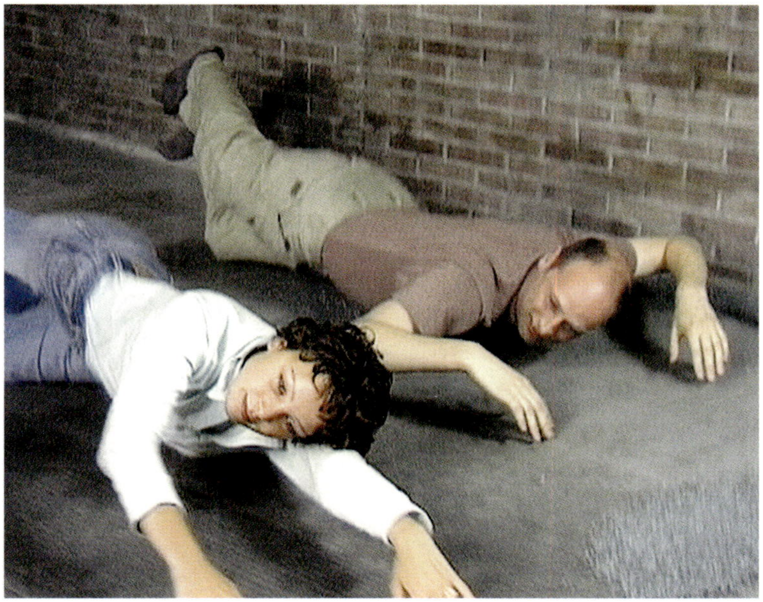

exhibition view 'Softer Catwalk in Collapsing Rooms', Galerie Gebauer, Berlin, 1999 and stills from video installation **Float**, 1998

Floating

Maxine Kopsa

[The camera shoots two actors on a set]

...I go down on my hands and knees, fall forward, turn only my head to the right and stretch my arms out on either side at about 45 degrees. I lie next to another who is also front down, face turned right, arms spread out to the side. I look passed the other head, passed it not at the gravel ground on which I lie, not at my own hand or arm. While I look, something falls onto the ground, close to me, sometimes on me...

The camera is indifferent to the scene unfolding before it – though perhaps it should be said now and I will come back to this later: the scene does not really 'unfold', it passes. Passes, detached. The viewer has little explanation to go on, little reassurance by way of familiar, and thus meaningful, behaviour of the actors or objects on the set. Like a foreign game for which the instruction manual is lost, this scene progresses, repeated, before the viewer as indifferently as it does before the camera.
Both the camera and the on-looker do just that: they look on. And during the first moments of his resigned contemplation, the viewer discerns a 'gap'. Initially he believes it is born of his own lack of perception or an intellectual flaw. So he stands watching, insulted, feeling stupid, left out of the plot. Until at some moment just before probable loss of interest and subsequent dismissal, he understands that he's meant to feel this gap. He is meant to feel the awkwardness. He is meant to feel an undetermined discomfort which isn't so easily resolved nor is it alleviated once named. This, for the reason that it's not purely 'foreign', simply 'alien', or obviously 'different'. This gap is the slow separation of act and meaning: a breach in the illusion of continuity. This gap is the distance between habit and sense and it is constructed on purpose: set into motion intentionally.

Writing it off as a gnawing sentiment or feeling of implausibility doesn't quite cover it though. It doesn't quite explain away the uneasiness. And it doesn't do it justice either.

Part one: The Accident

[Two figures lie on their front, in similar positions, parallel; next to them is a brick wall. The ground beneath them shakes back and forth and up and down... They move along with it, because of it, unable or unwilling to control movement while staring off into the distance, at nothing... Either as if unaware of their plight or unaffected by it, their expression is blank and they do not communicate. From time to time a substance falls from above them, like rain. They don't seem to notice...]

The most vital components, no: *basis*, for thought are incongruity and its more radical cousin, 'heterotopia'.[1] Together they form the requisite bedrock for everything creative. The start of all conception. – *Could this be the space in which Mik's work is moving?* – There's a system which stands and explains how things are and when it falls a new one can take its place but before this new matrix has been standardized its coordinates are blurry and messy. Out of this jumbled whole an institution finally arises, one which has been agreed upon, thus is seemingly based in logic, and followed through later by habit. It is governed ultimately by habitual thought and habitual action. DOG EQUALS DOG. It is within this system of conventions that the game of incongruity can be played: pretend for a moment that DOG EQUALS CAT. The institution isn't displaced by such a word game, its logic is merely suspended temporarily. A connection is made which doesn't make sense according to a specific reasoning (a dog is not a cat) but the disconnection within the agreement of the word (dog) being equal to the thing (dog) becomes obvious. The heterotopia, on the other hand, goes beyond the system, not to play *in* it but to play *with* it. DOG IS CAT. Instead of a further separation becoming clear between the term and the object, in a heterotopia a brave hand reaches out to attempt to bridge the distance and, in doing so, actually disorders the categories (the reasoning) put in place, namely 'word' and 'thing'.
Picture this for a moment:
Nomadic shepherds in South Ethiopia were observed to hold picture postcards sideways, so that the horizon was vertical.[2]
The heterotopia can disrupt only for a while – *can* only disrupt for a certain time: once the viewer is accustomed to the heterotopia, it becomes an incongruity.
The categories messed with being of course put in place by the conceded (read: artificial) institution; the gap being of course, by definition, unbridgeable.
For example:
You've been in a car accident and you were the driver. It was night. You decided last minute to go left at an intersection and moved too quickly into the turn lane. It was raining a little and the red car didn't see you soon enough and rear-ended you. It wasn't a bad accident and no one

was hurt but when you go back into the car and continue home you have a totally new view of Driving. You realize how difficult it is – or could be – to manoeuvre a machine 12 times a person's size, aware of all the other big cars on the road and all the other small people moving them. You're stunned by the fact that not everyone is bumping into one another constantly. Strange. Uncanny that we all learn this thing called driving and all do it so well and so consistently. And after the accident, for a short time, you see the convention called 'driving', you see it as an affected foreign throne and can't do it anymore. The system which worked – so smoothly, so naturally – becomes opaque and ridiculous. Not only the system we call traffic but also the machine itself. A 'steering wheel', four 'tires', two 'doors', 'seats', 'belts', 'gears', 'brake', 'left signal', 'lights'. It all falls apart, into separate, incongruous pieces.

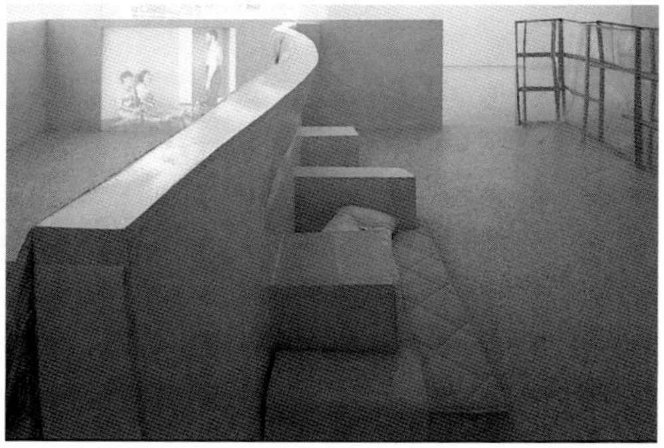

exhibition view Dutch Pavilion Venice Biennial, Venice, 1997, **Lick**, 1996, video installation

You've build up a system of behaviour or a tree of thought upon thought where all elements are consistent, each a logical step in a certain direction. You have to. And if you want to remain part of now, you continue building and branching off forever, 'now' being a good part of forever. Or you decide that it's complete (enough) and just swing from branch to branch basing – and so comparing – all new information to what is already categorized and thus resolved. Settled. Until you find yourself talking to X and you are both seated on a top branch. Both of you having climbed for a good while, carefully, not missing a crossing, watching out for the discrepancies. And you look down during a pause in the conversation and think: how did I get up here? All of a sudden the top branch, your seat, turns into an affected foreign throne, dislocated from the tree, and much too heavy to fly on its own.
You realize, lose control and drop.
That tree which you so precisely put together becomes an opaque, artificial construction; its structure, no longer transparent, which had determined your thoughts and your habits, becomes visible and absurd.
You land in Heterotopia.

But soon you forget the gap and get on with it (thankfully?). You regulate the distance between you and thing, decide on what to call it. And that's how you choose to see it (tame it), and you go on.

Part Two: DOG EQUALS DOG

[I watch questioningly as the two figures are being rolled around and bounced. The ground is shaking as well as the brick wall, sometimes slowly and then more aggressively. At times powder or dirt falls on the ground between them, in a kind of cadence with the moving of the legs, of the arms, of the wall. The pile it forms now bounces as well. Back and forth on the ground. Up and down up and down up and down, sometimes fast.]

An aside to consider the naturalness of 'our' method of (filmic) storytelling and the relativeness of convention. An illustration: a dark hotel room. The phone rings. The sound of a door shutting. A figure coming from the foreground moves into the background and picks up the receiver. 'Hello?' Pause. 'O.K., one hour.' Next scene. This same man sits at a table in a diner, across from another shorter man. It's night.

How much information has the director assumed we would infer? Quite a bit. We believe our man has just returned to his hotel. We presume this male character was called by the shorter man we see him seated with in the diner. We suppose this shorter man had phoned him to set up this meeting, 'in an hour'. We guess he went directly from his hotel room to the meeting. How natural is this? The scene has *unfolded* and we have assumed a progressive chronology. But has the viewer always deduced in such a manner? Have we always been blind to, or, allowed for, what can be called a 'missing link'?

Looking to the history of cinema we can see what the litter of missing links has left behind. And if we parallel the development of cinema to our development of perception we might come closer to a glimpse of convention-at-work, or a brief sketch of the rupture.

The Institutional Mode of Representation (IMR) – note: an *institution* – appeared approximately thirty years after cinema began, sometime after 1906.[3] It was a closed system of stable and thus recognizable 'symbols' of representation in the medium of film. It continues today. Before this there was... what? According to some film theorists, the whole of film before IMR did have a general bond and this connection could be referred to as PMR (Primitive Mode of Representation) – a different *type* of institution but an institution nevertheless. The fact that it is referred to as 'primitive' suggests two things. The first is a theory of continuous evolution, the second, going further, implies a comparison with the stage that comes after it: if early cinema is called primitive then we assume that it is less developed than the system of narration which is no longer termed primitive, following it. And by saying this we assume that the two have matching intentions, thereby erasing the missing links (incongruities) in an historical tale. But we know better:

The emblematic symbolism of early cinema has obviously turned inward and has been extended beyond the moment. The literal movements or gestures became figurative, psychological. We have become accustomed to a certain *language* in the narrative of film, one which has not always existed. One to which we have so efficiently adapted that it has become difficult to see it as such: as a *learned* structure and as just one possibility of perception. For instance, the 'cinema of attractions'[4] (a more recent term for 'primitive cinema') denotes a connection with a fun-fair or circus, inferring the scenes of early cinema have more to do with displaying novelty than developing a story-line. Attractions implies a displaying of 'experience', of 'moments of spectacle' which engage the spectator explicitly instead of making of him a voyeur.[5] There is no will to keep the viewer in suspense, the intention instead is to surprise him and to do this by way of the power of the moment. Not through an extension or suspension of

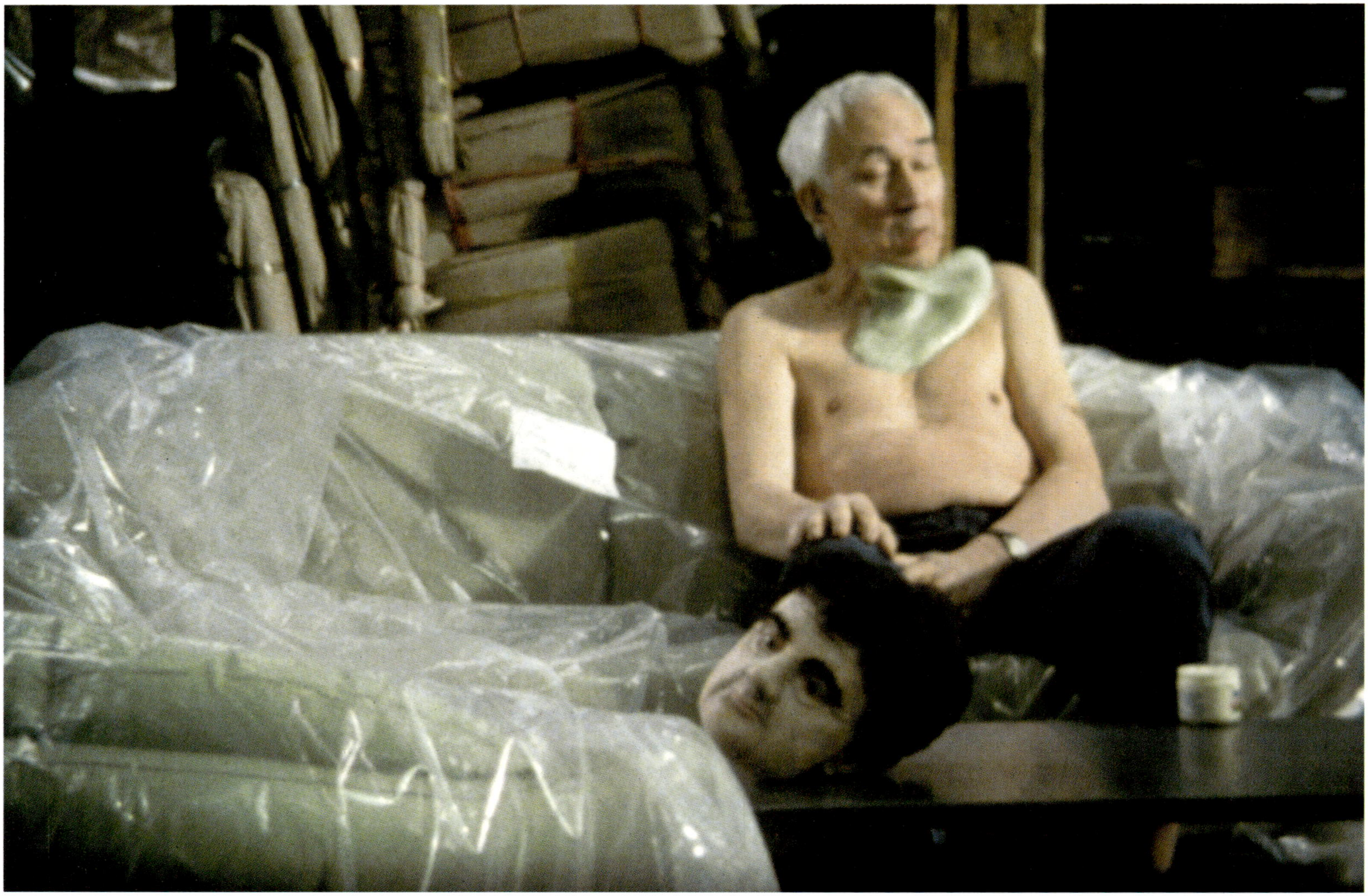

 stills from video installation **Fluff**, 1996

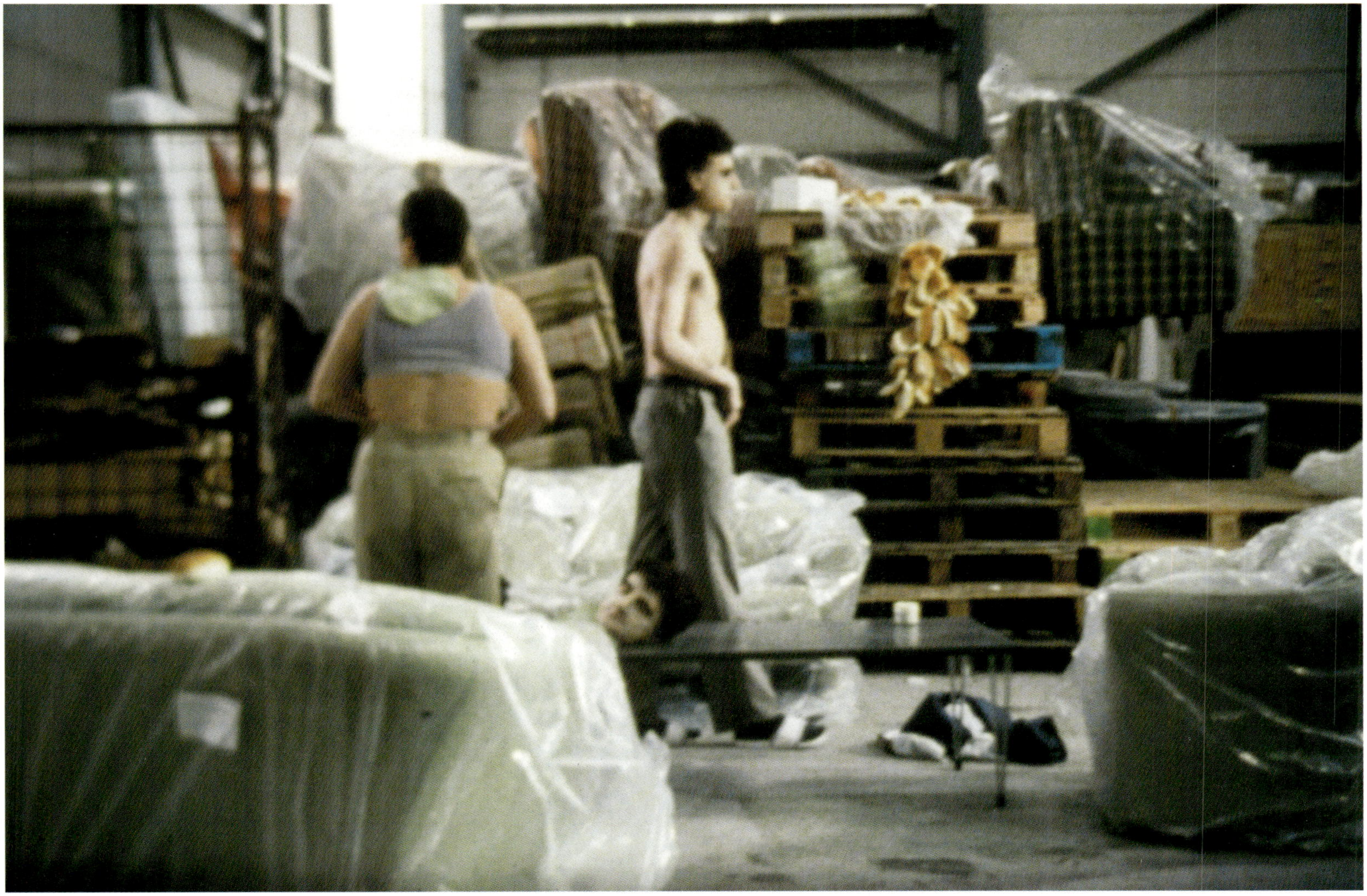

the (now expected) denouement. So enters into our story the decisive factor of time. It is this element of time, of *progression*, which is the most apparent difference between early and later cinema, proving their contrary intentions. An early film would start and finish almost randomly, often when the film itself simply ran out. No beginning or end, no build-up, no climax. No editing. The camera was often still, horizontal, there were no close-ups, no need because the character was not of central significance. The language was one of gestures, the focus on external behaviourism. All of these factors added up make for a genre of cinema which is entirely unlike our concept of movie. More than that, such a film seems to us now, unnatural, not realistic and full of missing links. In this sense, almost *Mikkean*: the scenes passing before a detached camera. No glue seemingly intended.

So what would be the relevant climax regarding the then and now of storytelling, and how does it pertain to the gap? One possibility: The missing links or ruptures in storytelling have existed in various forms always, but only become obvious with hindsight, once the structure of the narrative is laid bare. We have become used to a story with a beginning and an end and one without needless repetition and, as a consequence, we project this edited perception (of representation) onto the world around us and attempt to live it. Our reality is glued together by our fiction – it probably always has been – but even if we know this we cannot dismiss it or correct it: not while we're still standing in the tale. In the present, missing links are blind spots.

Part three: DOG IS CAT

Aernout Mik seems to know we became used to a story with a beginning, a middle and an end and one without needless repetition. That, as a consequence, we project this edited perception (of representation) onto the world around us. And better: that our reality is formed by our fiction (convention) and that we are consistent to avoid incongruity. To avoid madness. He knows, but he offers us not a build-up of these beliefs but their exposure. He breaks down elements of normality one by one, stripping away at convention. But never disregarding it absolutely and never transgressing into chaos. He shows our institutions denied of their logical significance, and does so indifferently: The camera does not enter into dialogue, the scene passes, detached, as do the figures. The whole, absurd, *primitive*.

[Am I watching a habit? A ritual? Neurosis? Could a habit be considered a personal ritual? A procedure. Repeated. Repeated so often that it becomes a neurotic tick?
What does absurd mean... what are the metaphysics of absurdism? Is it not the poetics of the gap? Thus: everything. Word and thing and how they do and do not connect depending on one's perception; the meaning therefore of the world around us. Or, in this case, getting the whole relative picture and (not always) knowing the difference between a habit, a ritual, a

neurosis, or: (not always) seeing the separation of meaning and act, cat and dog. Sometimes the distinction is blurred but it never dissolves.]

The funny thing is these institutions Mik reveals are ones we have made up ourselves: we've made up the rules and have subsequently subjected ourselves to them... We go through the motions in our projected reality and can forget to accept the inconsistencies which belong to it, becoming, in times of doubt, an enemy of your own state. Believing too strongly that the structure is real, real even outside of our thoughts.

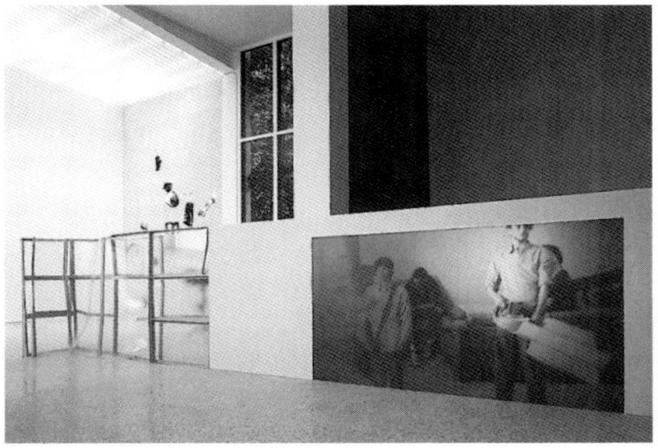

exhibition view Dutch Pavilion Venice Biennial, Venice, 1997, **Suck**, 1997, video installation

[I look back at the projected video: the figures appear inanimate, like objects without acquired meaning; their movements abstracted from their situation, slowed; their gestures dissociated from their own body. I watch this strange routine and nonetheless start to anticipate when the grime will fall again. I look and start to predict when the aggressive parts will follow. I learn to expect their movements. It becomes a domesticated rhythm... And once I begin to understand that the rhythm of the gestures of these two figures is repeated, I start looking for differences.
I observe their movements more closely. The question 'why?' I began with, disappears...
I adapt. What at first seemed foreign and forced becomes logical... no... logical is the wrong word. Inexplicably familiar is better. Now I sense the workings of this gap, as if intuitively.
The structure is laid open but is no longer exclusive.
Why was the scene alien to begin with?... because it didn't seem *normal* for two figures to undergo something offensive without reacting... They did not communicate, not between themselves and not to us... It was as if their bodies were separated from their minds, or reason, and they simply *underwent*. Absurd, perhaps, from the perception of an individual convinced that we act and re-act according to outside influences. We do, mostly. Absurd to one who believes the world and its stories are made up of cause and effect.
Now I see the band aid holding the whole thing together. Dog – band aid – cat; cause – band aid – effect.]

We may project consistently and, so, ruthlessly, but as mentioned above, we do occasionally see through the necessary nonsense of our own daily rituals. Thankfully.
Aernout Mik seems to play with the necessity of the nonsense, with the presence of codification in our vision of reality. He doesn't displace it, he realizes its necessity and questions it... or, more precisely: makes it visible. We're not sitting on the top branch talking to X, we're looking up at the tree after falling to the ground and we're considering whether or not to start climbing anew. At the same time we know we will. We will get up grab the first branch and ascend to the top only to drop once we've reached it again. Bruised and stunned but without any choice we start all over. Climbing, swinging, falling.

CAT EATS DOG

...My whole body is bouncing sideways and upwards and down. I fall back sometimes onto my hip and then it too goes up into the air. Up and down and up and down up and down. The head of the person in front of me is moving and bumping on the ground. We don't stop really, sometimes we go slower though and then all of a sudden faster and then my elbows knock the floor. My hips up in the air, and then hers. Mine back down...We lie here perpetually. I don't remember why.

1
Michel Foucault, *The Order of Things*, Random House, Inc., New York (1994, first published in 1971), p. xviiff

2
Quoted from JCJ Vanderheyden in his catalogue from Museum Boymans-van Beuningen, Rotterdam, 1990.

3
Noël Burch, *Life to Those Shadows*, University of California Press, Berkeley, 1990, p. 186ff

4
The term was coined by Tom Gunning and André Gaudreault in the 1980s, see: Richard Abel (ed.), *Silent Film*, Rutgers University Press, New Jersey, 1995, p. 72-82

5
op cit., p.75

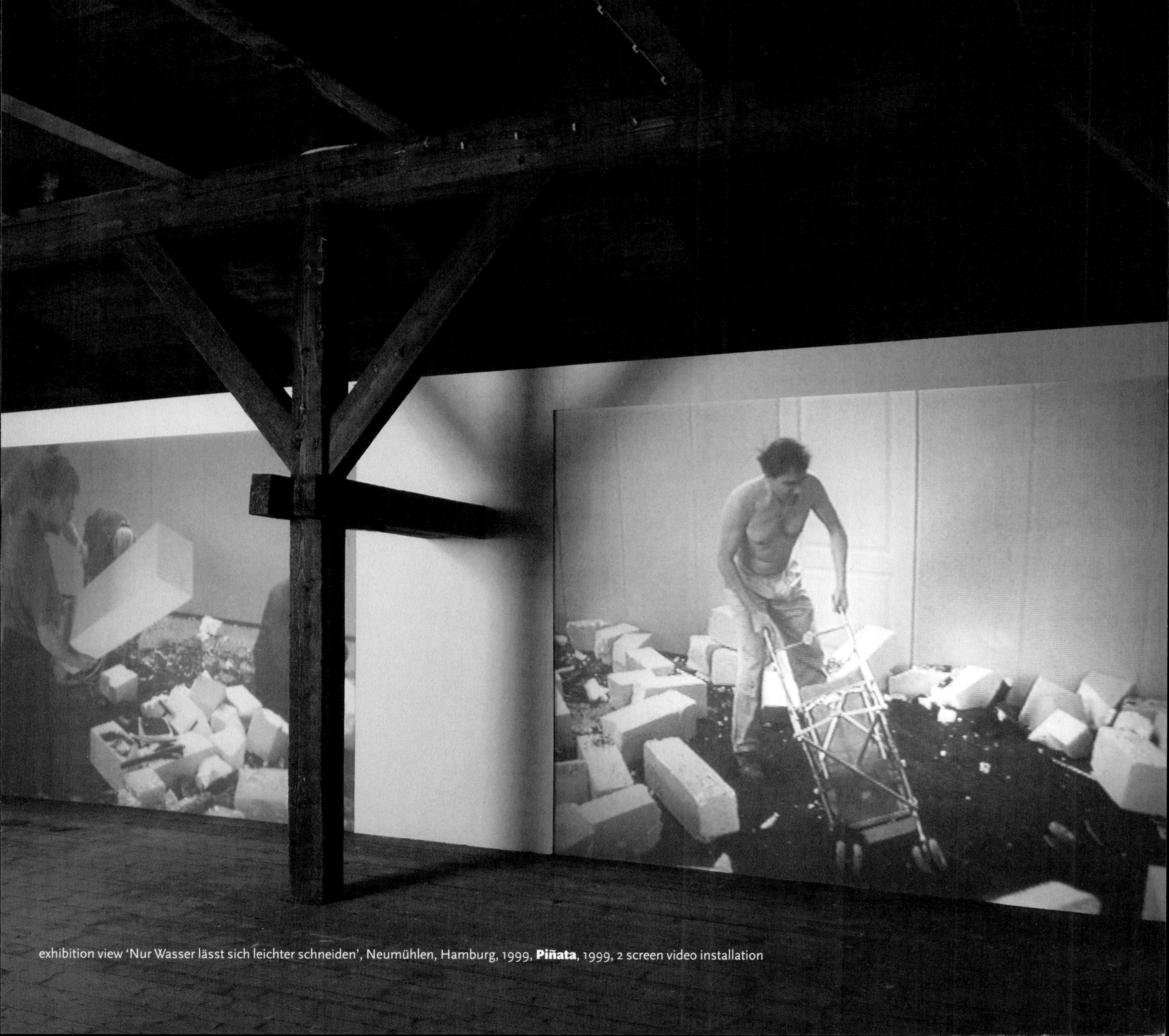

exhibition view 'Nur Wasser lässt sich leichter schneiden', Neumühlen, Hamburg, 1999, **Piñata**, 1999, 2 screen video installation stills from video installation **Piñata**, 1999

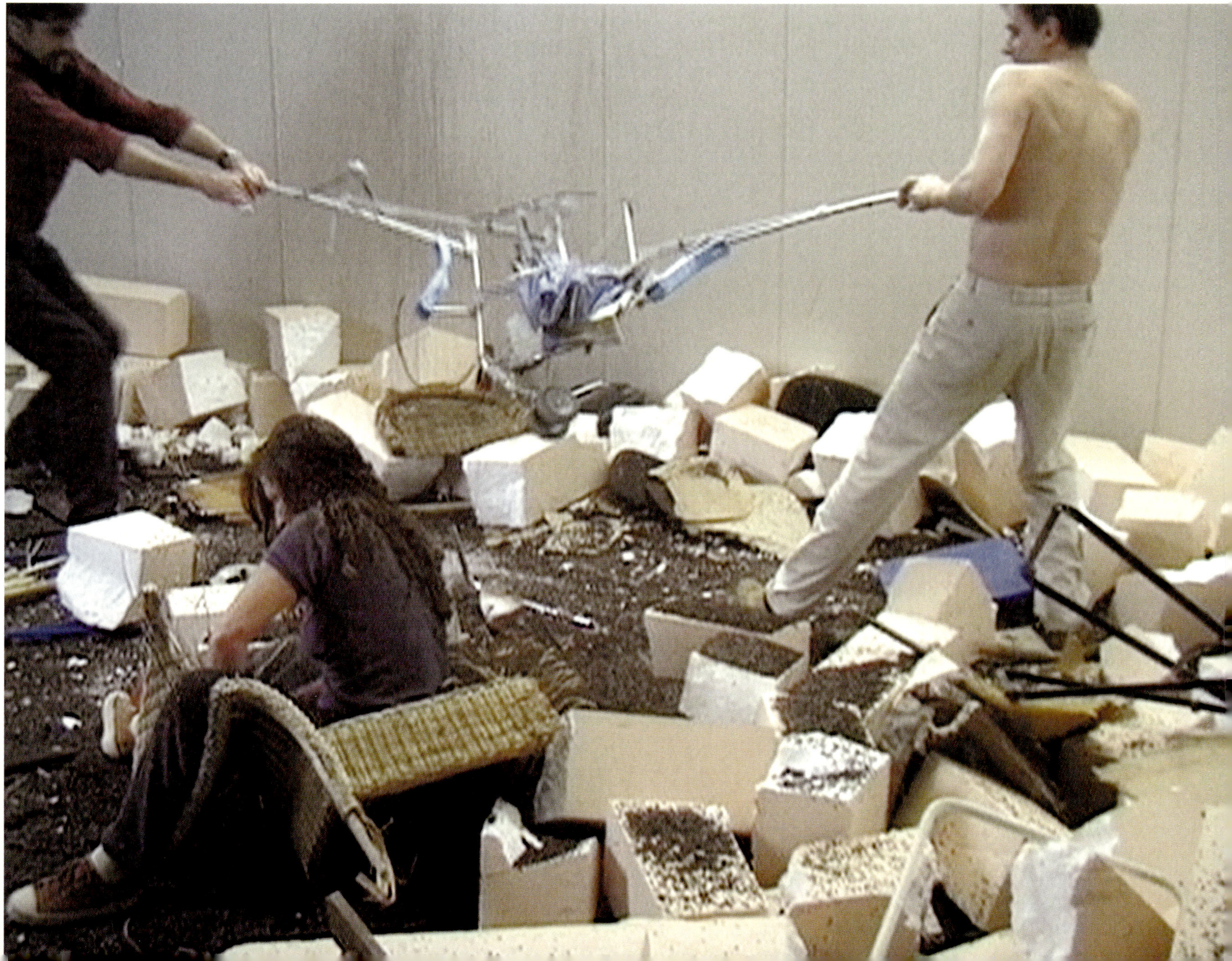

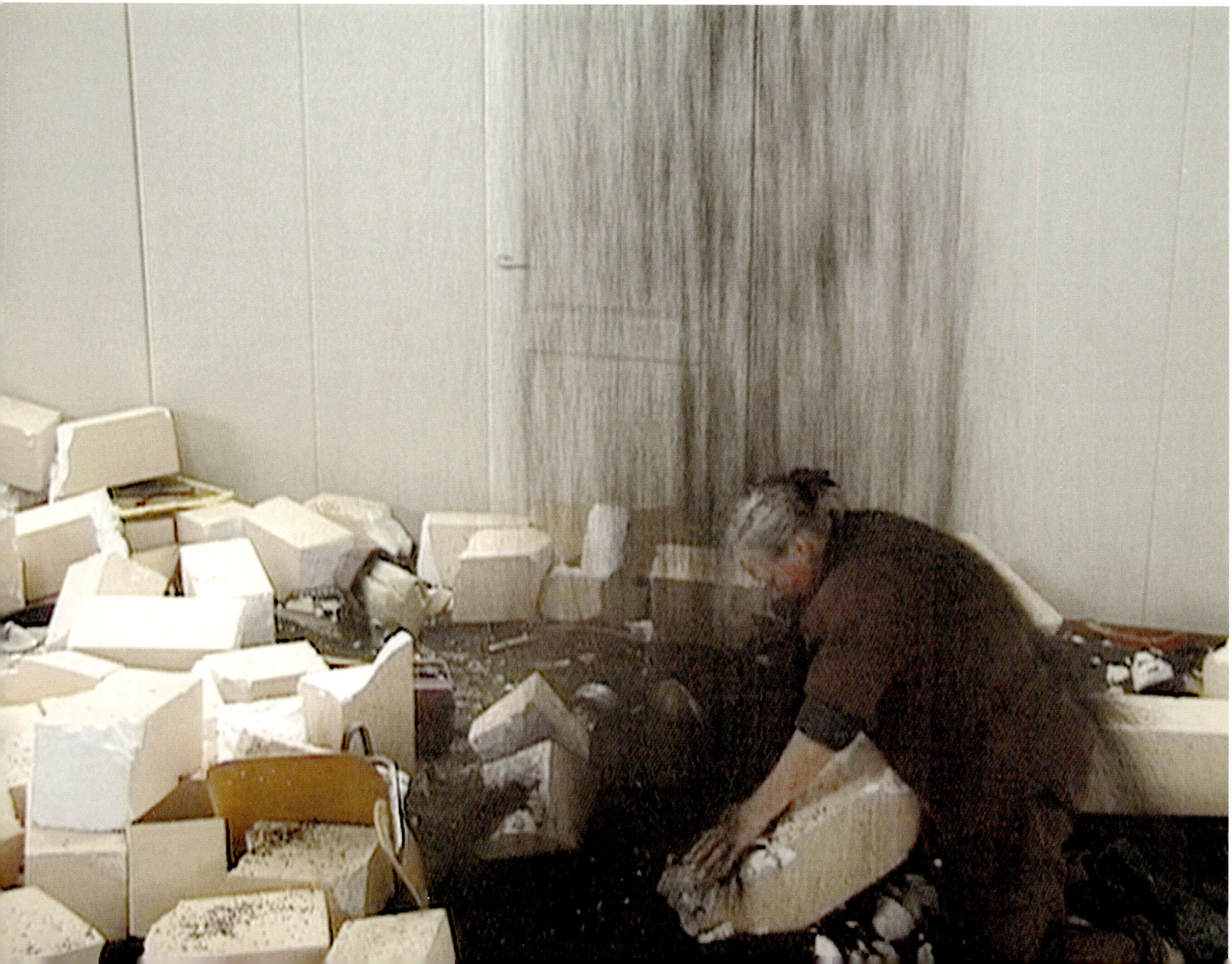

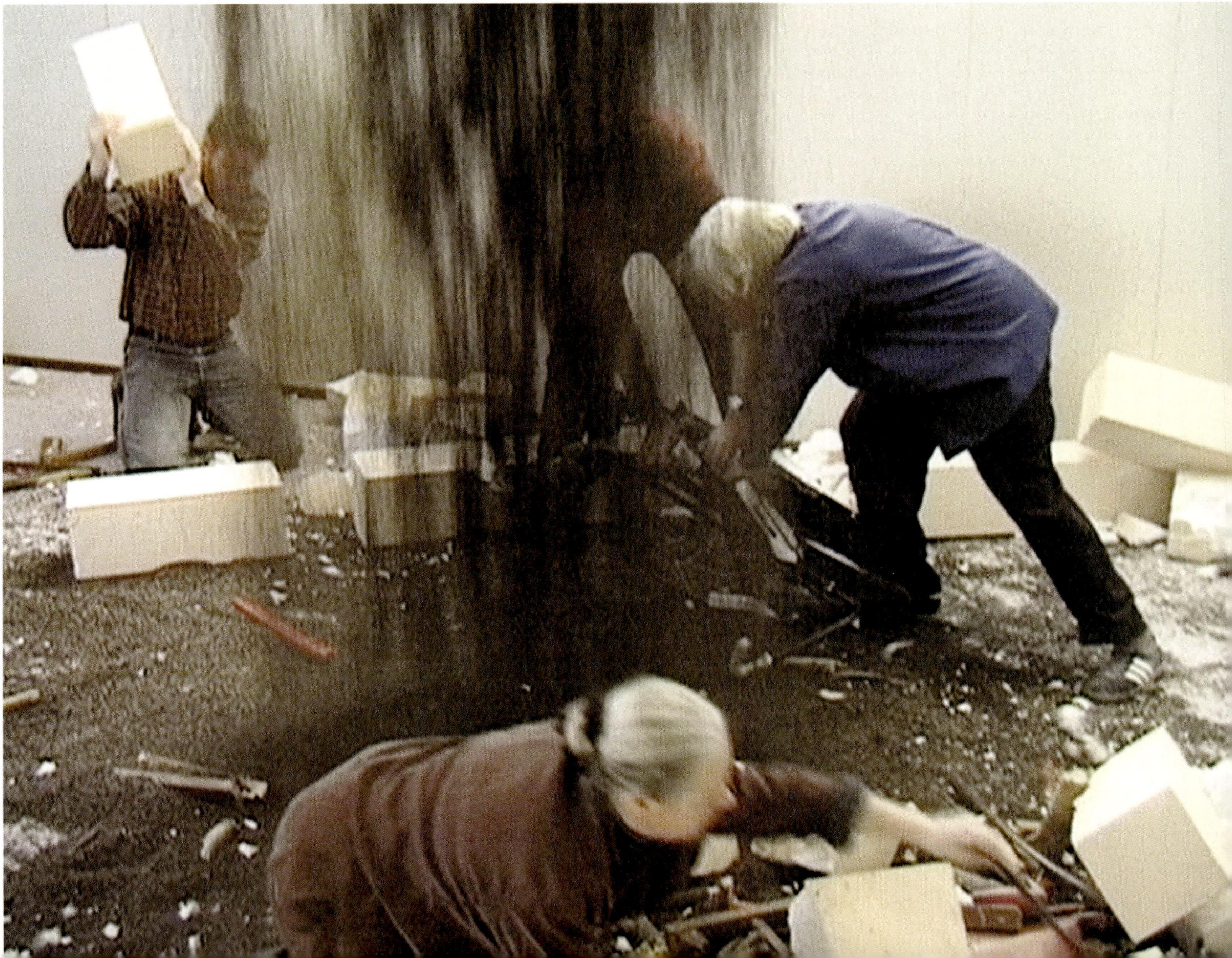

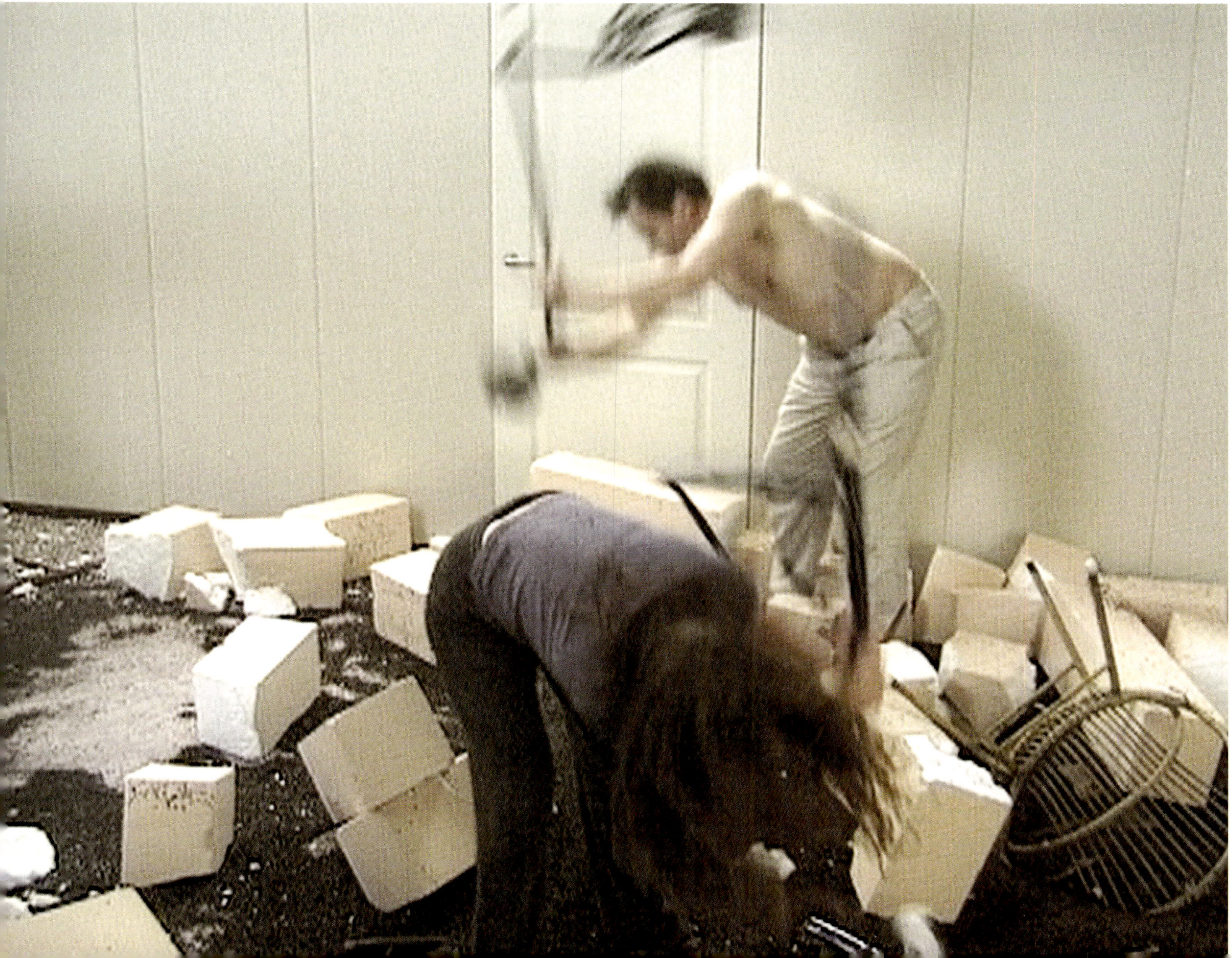

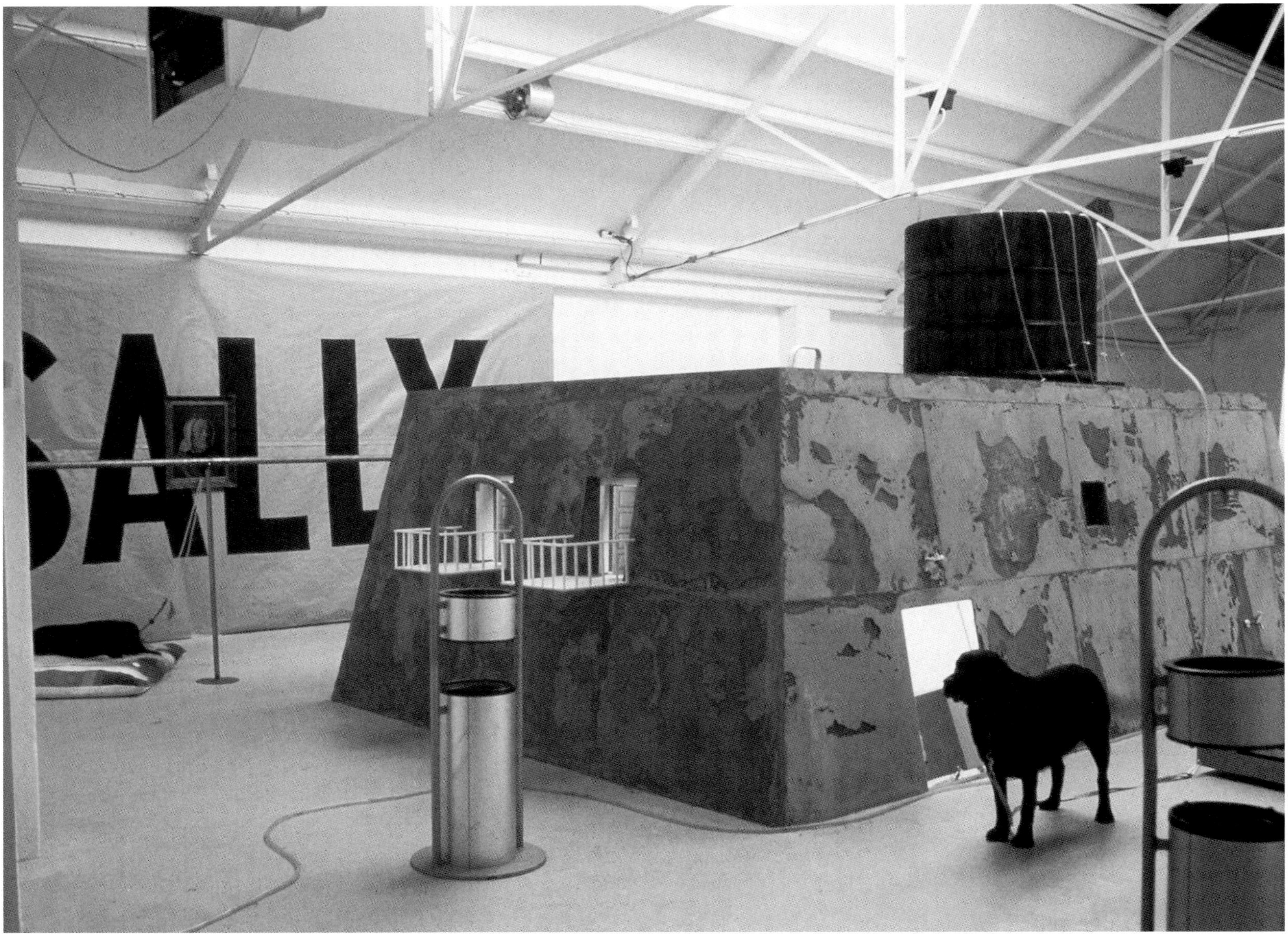

 exhibition view Galerie Fons Welters, Amsterdam, 1992, **The Philosophy of Furniture**, 1992, Adam Kalkin and Aernout Mik, mixed media installation

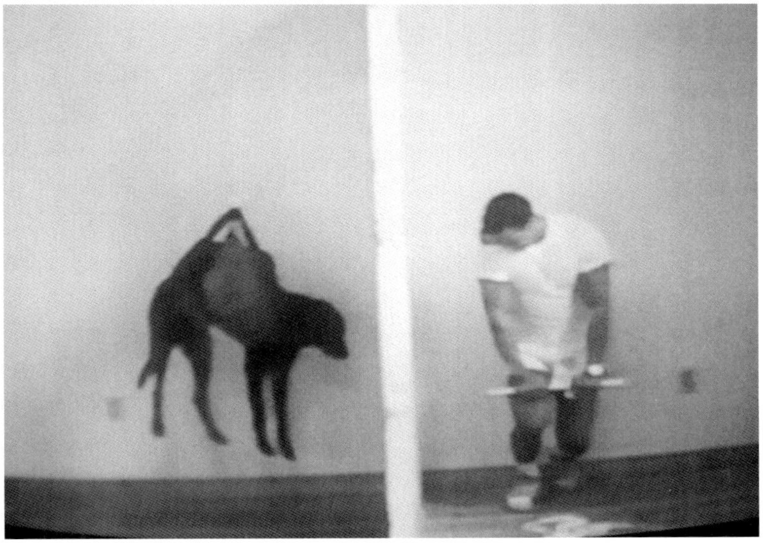

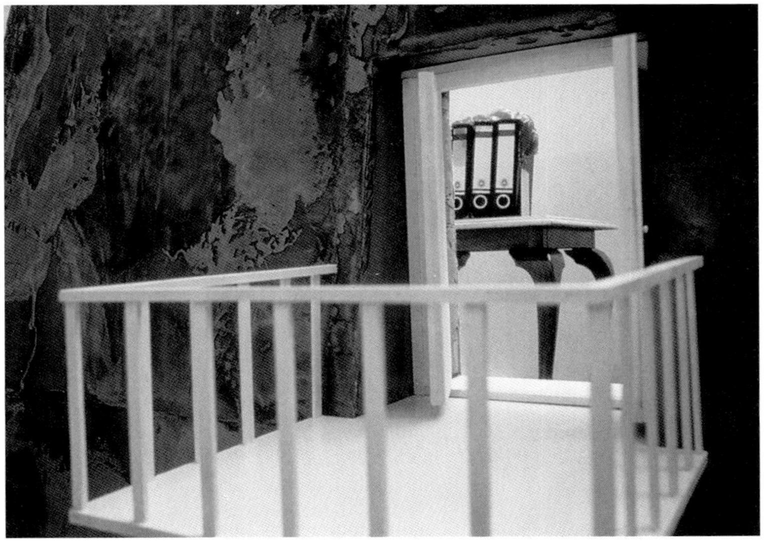

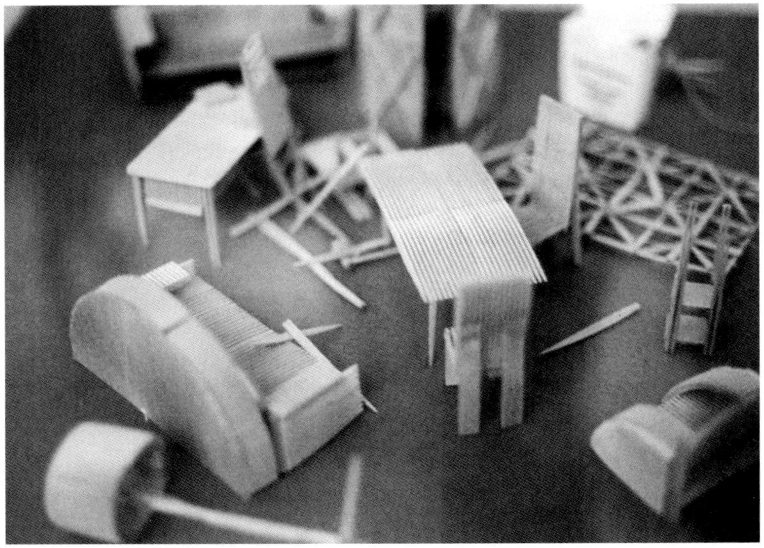

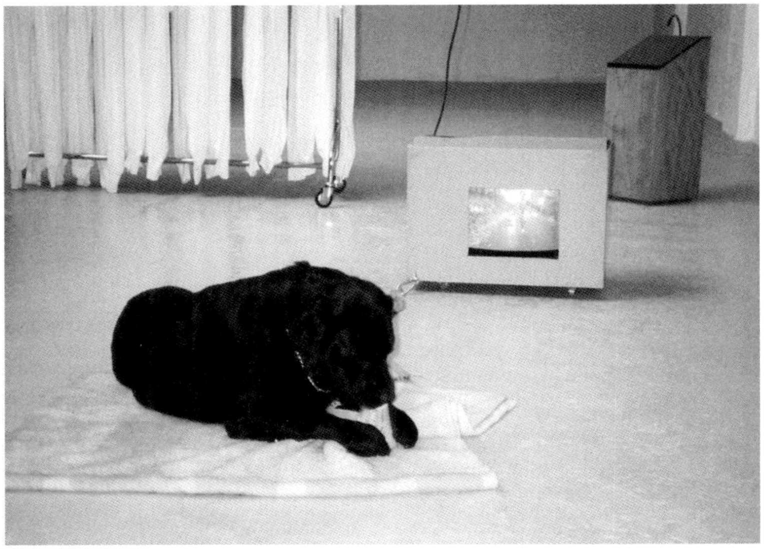

The Philosophy of Furniture, 1992 (details)

a small head, 1998, live installation at Triple X festival, Amsterdam, 1998

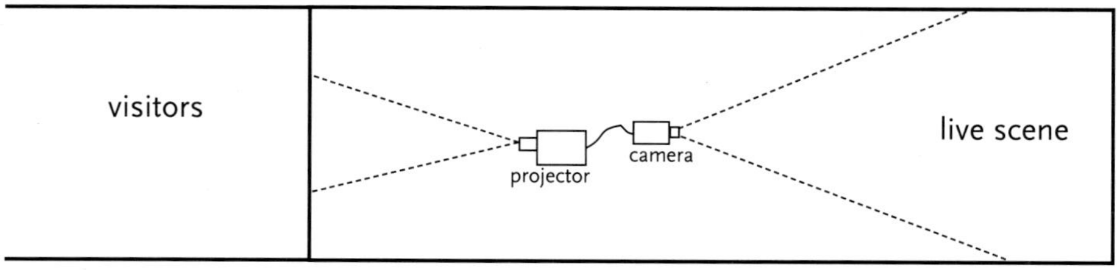

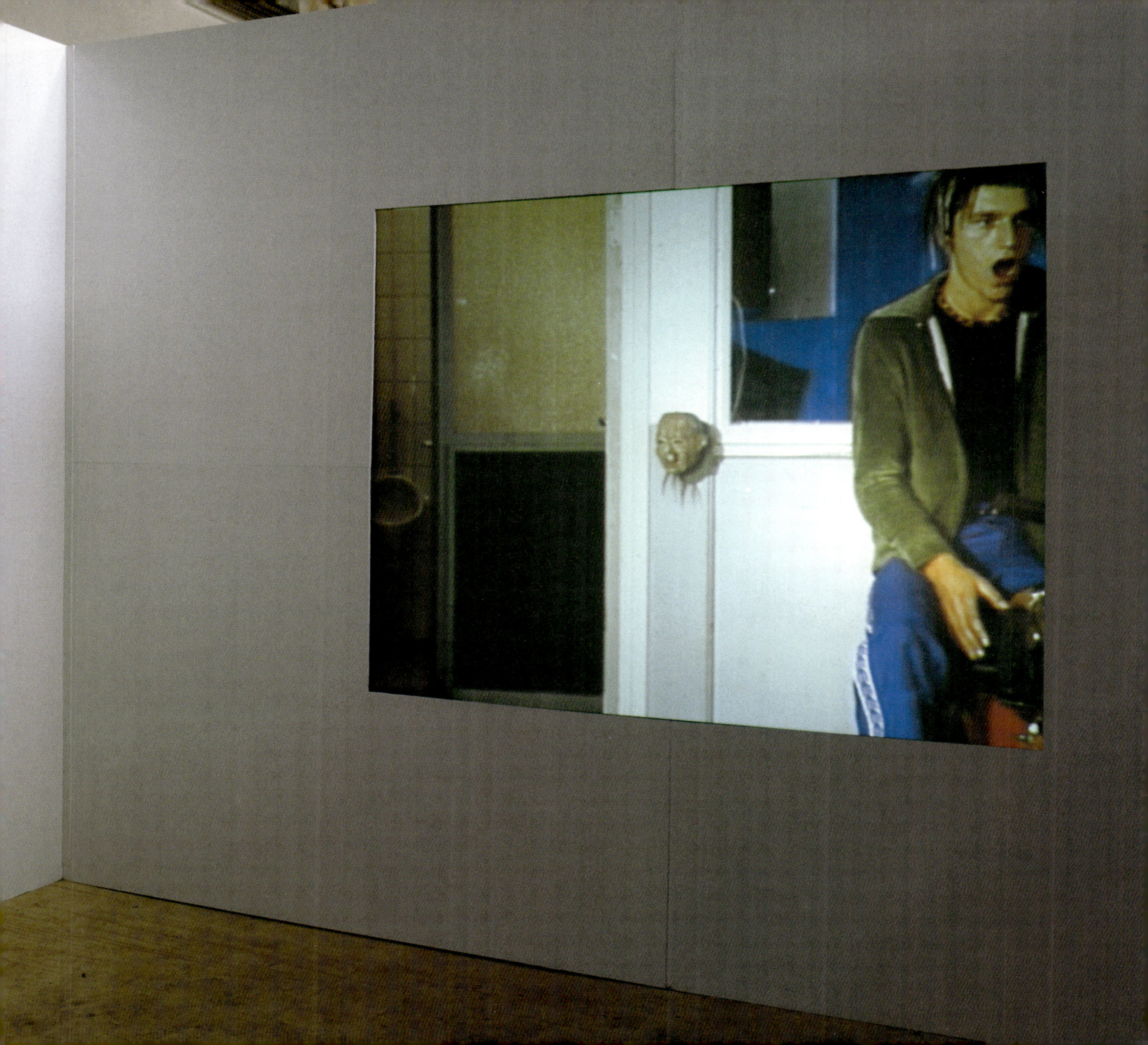

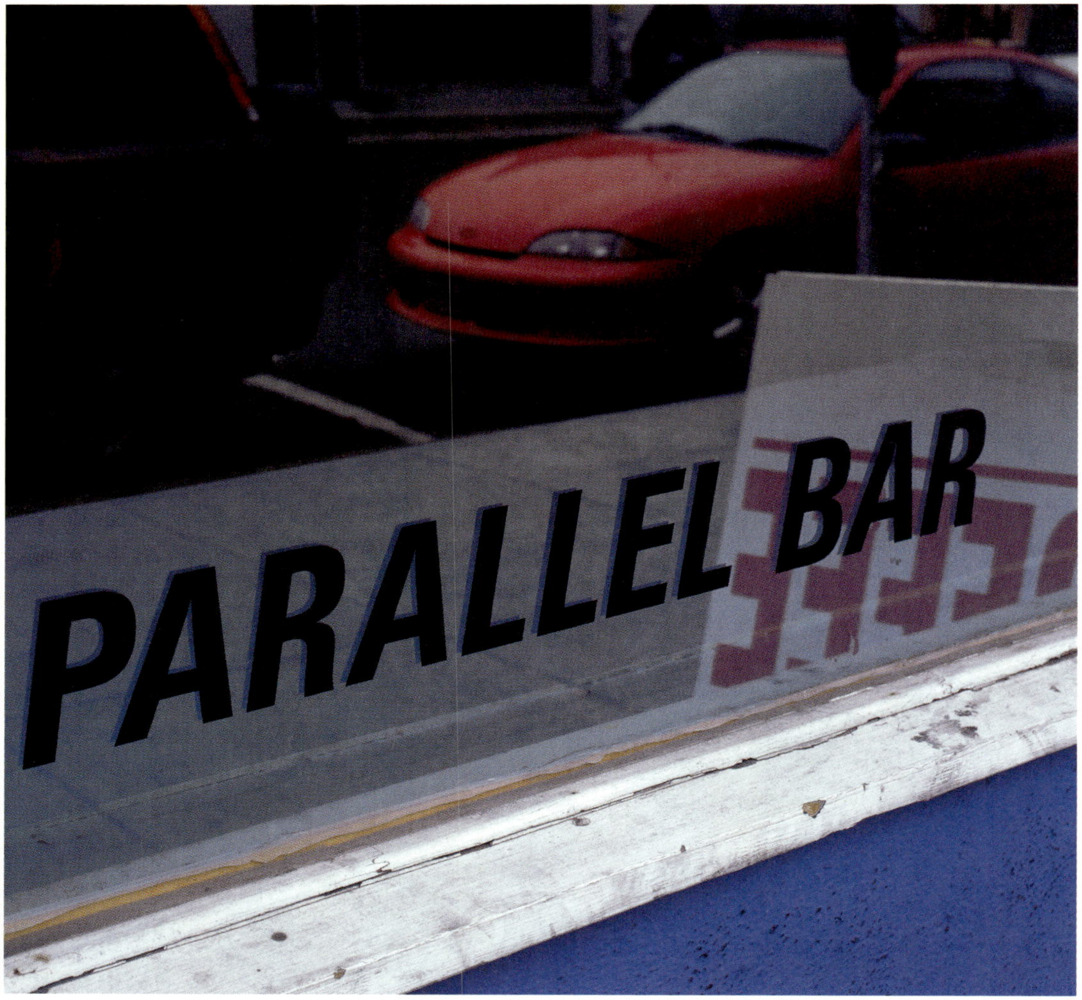

Parallel Bar, 1999, live installation at the exhibition 'In All the Wrong Places', Ottawa, 1999

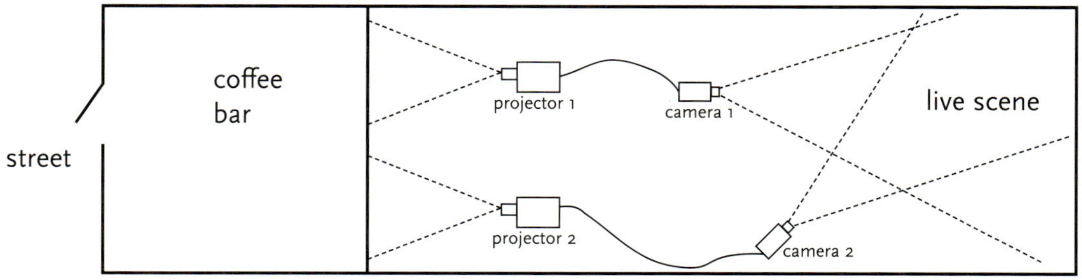

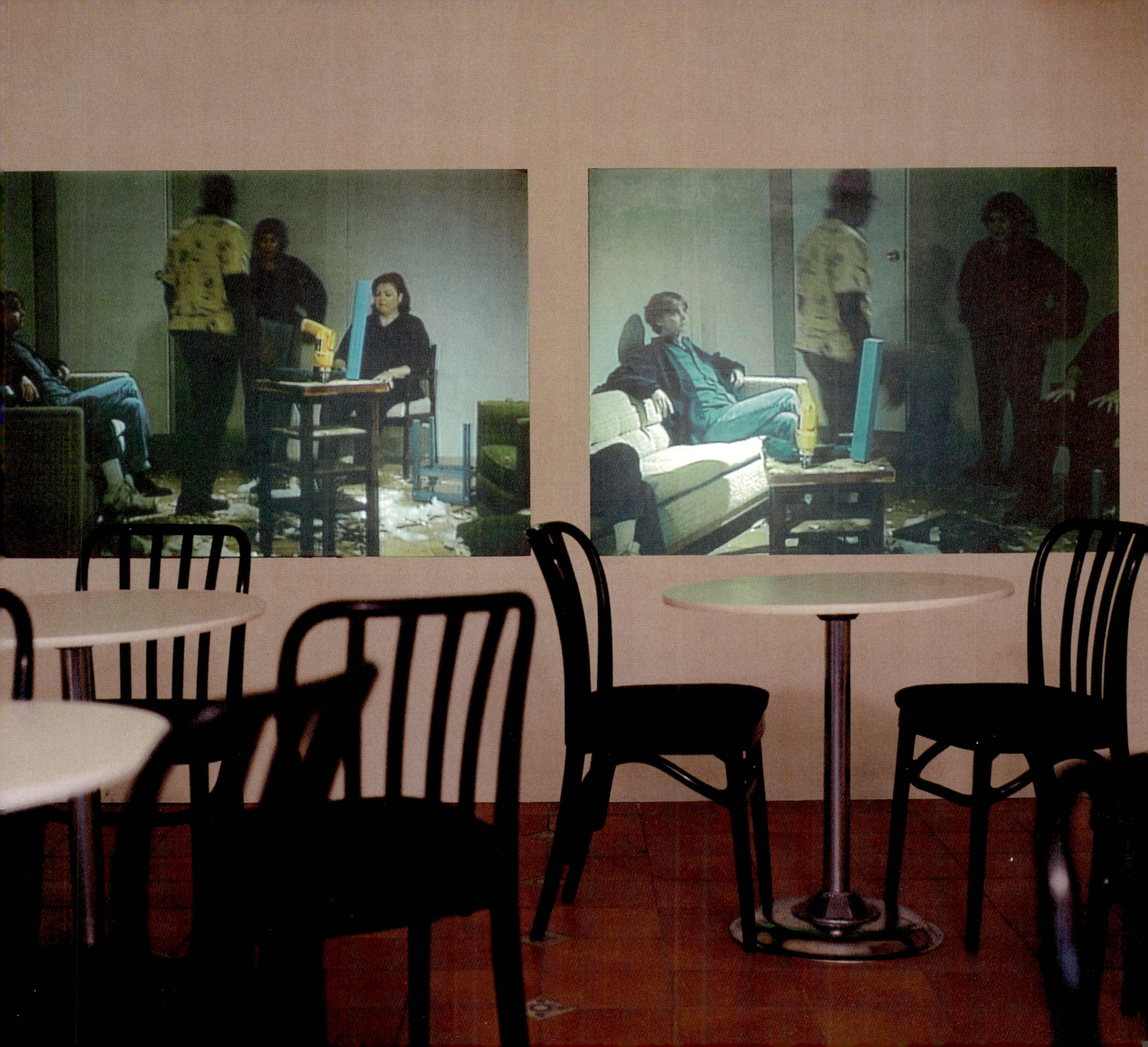

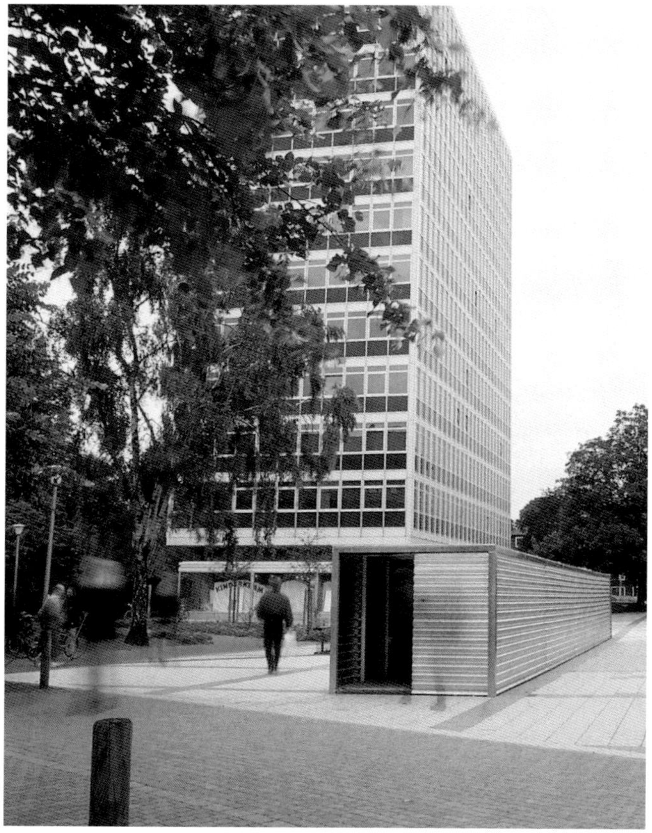

langer oder liegender Affe, 1996, live installation at the exhibition 'Abendland', Munster, 1996

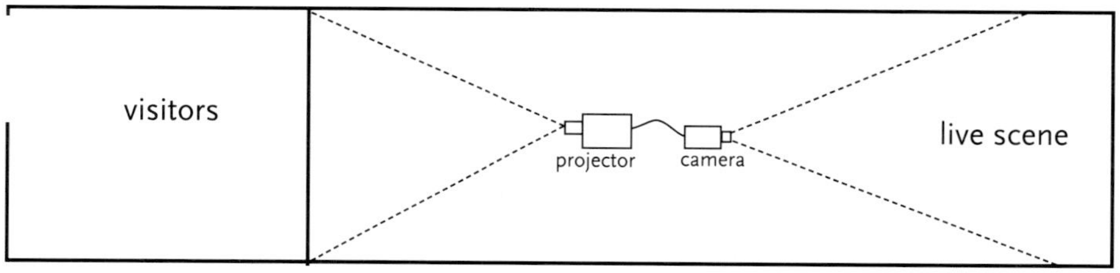

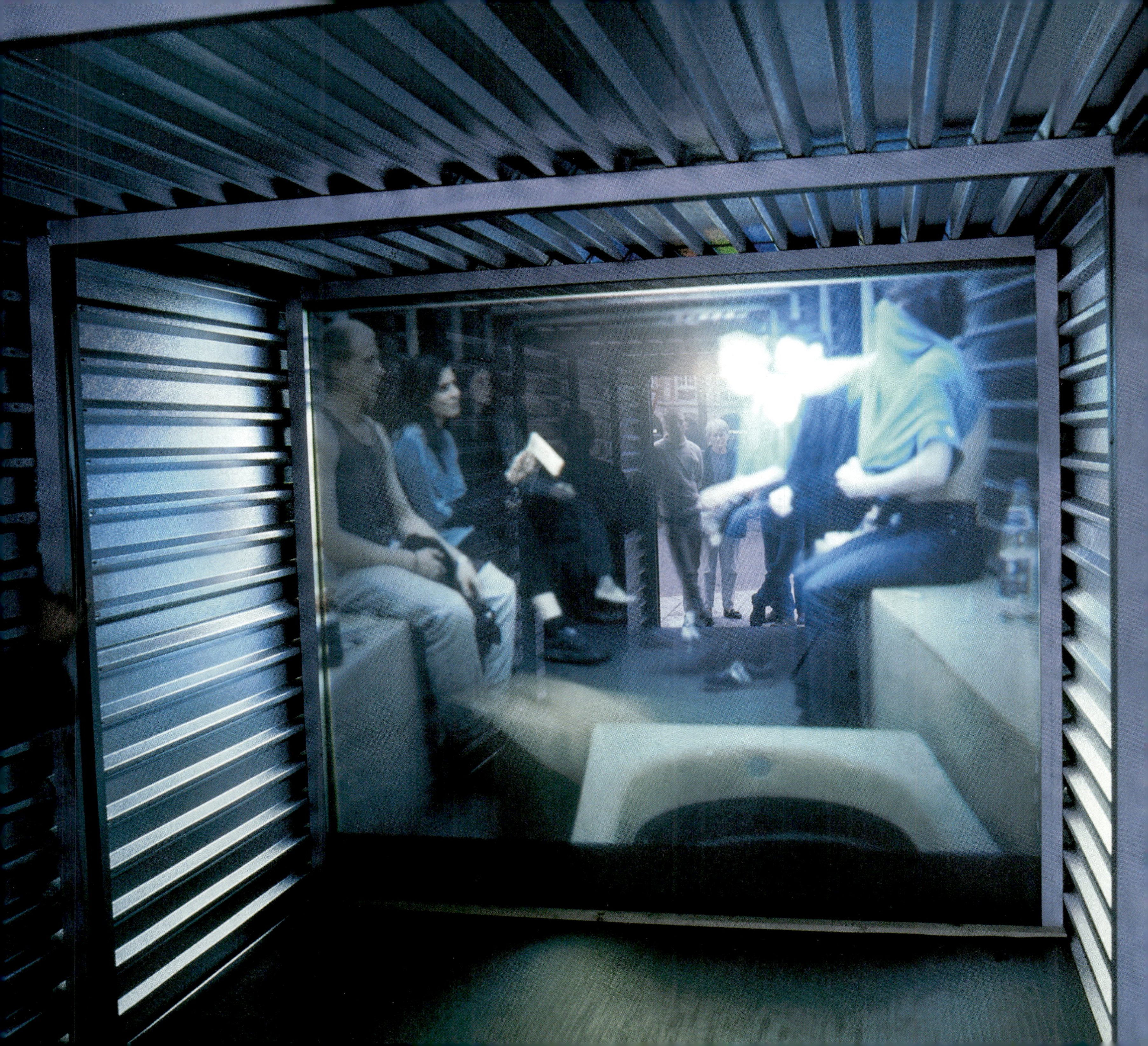

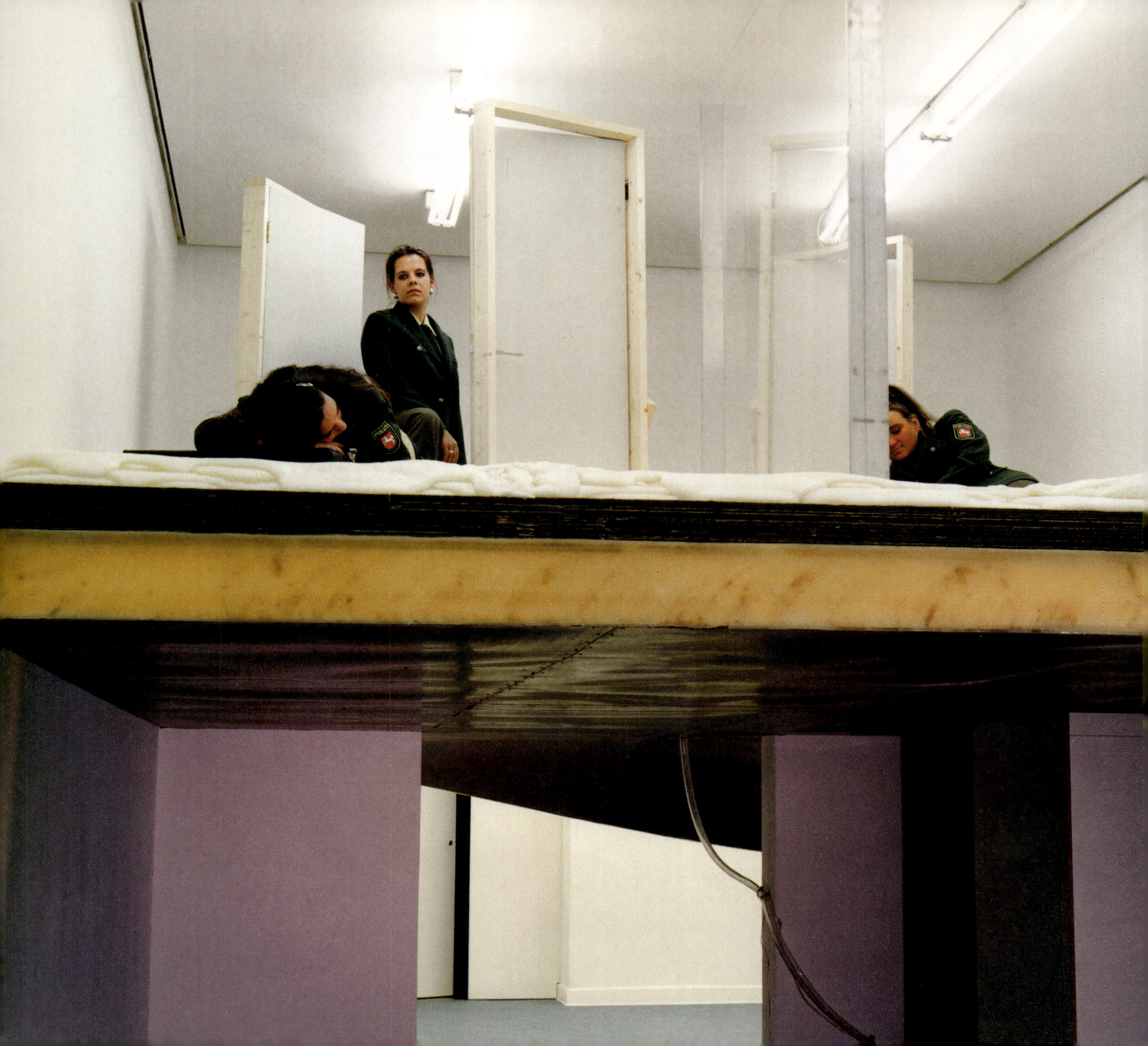

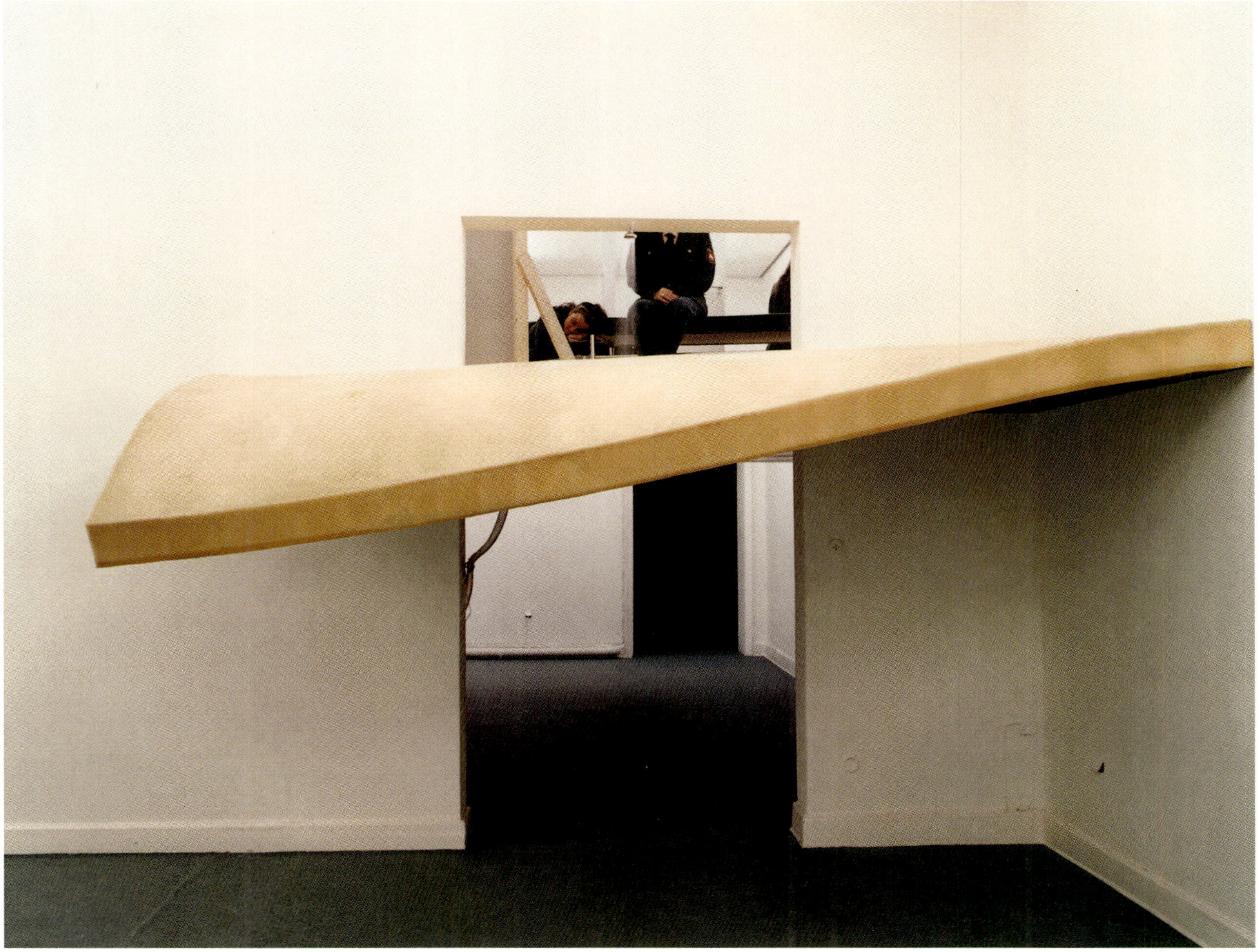

Wie die Räume gefüllt werden müssen, 1995, live installation at the exhibition 'Preis des Kunstvereins Hannover', Kunstverein Hannover, Hanover, 1995

List of works

P. 2-3
Aap, 1998
interactive robot, mixed media installation
commisioned by Sint Maartenskliniek, Nijmegen
and Praktijkburo, Amsterdam

P. 6
Für Nichts und Wieder Nichts, 1992
mixed media installation

P. 7
Assistant (from **Für Nichts und Wieder Nichts**),
1992
inkjet on fabric, filling
size c. 180 x 40 x 50 cm
collection Deweer Art Gallery, Otegem (B)

P. 9, 54
a small group, falling, 1998
video installation
mastered on digi beta from dv
loop
edition 2

P. 12-13, 78
Lick, 1996
video installation
mastered on digi beta from dv
loop
edition 2

P. 14-17, 21
Mob, 1998
video installation
mastered on digi beta from dv
loop
edition 2

P. 18, 24-26
Garage, 1998
video installation
mastered on digi beta from dv
loop
edition 2

P. 19, 80-81
Fluff, 1996
video installation
mastered on digi beta from s-16 mm film
loop
edition 2

P. 20
Modderbank, 1997
2 couches, pump, timer, mud
size c. 500 x 120 x 80 cm

P. 22-23
Swab, 1999
video installation
mastered on digi beta from dv
loop
edition 2

P. 28-31
Softer Catwalk in Collapsing Rooms, 1999
video installation
mastered on digi beta from dv
loop
edition 2
collection Stedelijk Museum, Amsterdam;
De Vleeshal, Middelburg

P. 32-33, 83
Suck, 1997
video installation
mastered on digi-beta from dv
loop
edition 2
collection Stedelijk Van Abbemuseum, Eindhoven

P. 34-36, 38
Kitchen, 1997
video installation
mastered on digi beta from dv
loop
edition 2
collection Stedelijk Museum, Amsterdam

P. 41
Portrait, 1998
colour photograph on aluminium
size 135 x 110 cm
edition 3
collection Het Domein, Sittard; Koninklijke PTT Nederland, Den Haag

P. 43-53
Hongkongoria, 1997-1998
Marjoleine Boonstra and Aernout Mik
video installation, 7 projections
mastered on digi beta from dv
loops
edition 2

P. 57
two men, floating, 1999
inkjet on inflatable
size c. 15 x 5 x 4 m

P. 61
Project for Conference Center La Vie, 1993
live installation
beds, sleepers, lights, furniture, hamsters

P. 62-63
3 laughing and 4 crying, 1998
video installation
mastered on digi-beta from dv
loop
edition 2

P. 65-71
Territorium, 1999
video installation, 2 synchronized projections
mastered on digi beta from dv
loops
edition 2

P. 72-73
Blue Sinkhole, 1995
live installation
guards, fake guards, mixed media

P. 74-75
Float, 1998
video installation
mastered on digi beta from dv
loop
edition 2

P. 85-89
Piñata, 1999
video installation, 2 synchronized projections
mastered on digi beta from dv
loops
edition 2

P. 90-91
The Philosophy of Furniture, 1992
Adam Kalkin and Aernout Mik
installation, dogs, mixed media

P. 92-93
a small head, 1998
live installation
slowly zooming in and out camera, live video projection, rear projection screen, division walls, actors, field beds, mopeds, Chinese head

P. 94-95
Parallel Bar, 1999
live installation
coffee bar, division wall, rear projection screens, slowly zooming in and out cameras, live video projections, actors, furniture, drills

P. 96-97
langer oder liegender Affe, 1996
live installation
camera, live video projection, rear projection screen, plexiglass, actors, benches, moving cardboard box, bath, rattles

P. 98-99
Wie die Räume gefüllt werden müssen, 1995
live installation
actors, mixed media

P. 103
Stuffed, Weak and Filthy, 1995
s-16 mm film projection on plexiglass, couches
edition 2

P. 104
Miscellaneous Exits for Smaller Animals, 1991
mixed media sculpture
size c.123 x 515 x 102 cm
collection Stedelijk Van Abbemuseum, Eindhoven

P. 107
A Hundred Times, 1994
live installation
actors, puppets, plastic curtains, small objects, gymnasium

Aernout Mik

1962
Born in Groningen

Education
1983-1988
Academie Minerva, Groningen
1987-1988
Ateliers '63, Haarlem

Prizes
1993
Preis des Kunstvereins Hannover
1998
Sandbergprijs, Amsterdams Fonds voor de Kunst

Lives and works in Amsterdam

Solo exhibitions (a selection)

1990
Voorwerk, Witte de With, Rotterdam
1992
Für Nichts und Wieder Nichts, Deweer Art Gallery, Otegem (B) (cat.)
The Philosophy of Furniture, Galerie Fons Welters, Amsterdam (with Adam Kalkin)
1995
Mommy, I'm sorry, De Vleeshal, Middelburg (with Adam Kalkin)
Wie die Räume gefüllt werden müssen, Kunstverein Hannover, Hanover (cat.)
Stuffed, Weak and Filthy, Deweer Art Gallery, Otegem (B) (cat.)
1997
XLVII Biennale di Venezia: Padiglione Olandese, Venice (with Willem Oorebeek) (cat.)
1998
Galeri Index, Stockholm
Hongkongoria, Stedelijk Van Abbemuseum, Eindhoven (with Marjoleine Boonstra) (cat.)
1999
small disasters, Galerie Fons Welters, Amsterdam
Softer Catwalk in Collapsing Rooms, Galerie Gebauer, Berlin
Piñata, Deweer Art Gallery, Otegem (B)
2000
primal gestures, minor roles, Stedelijk Van Abbemuseum, Eindhoven (cat.)
Kasseler Kunstverein, Kassel

Group exhibitions (a selection)

1987
Capital Gains, 't Venster, Rotterdam
1988
Een Grote Activiteit / A Great Activity, Stedelijk Museum, Amsterdam (cat.)
1989
Mik-Leijenaar-Strik, Museum 't Kruithuis, 's-Hertogenbosch (cat.)
1990
Capital Gains, Museum Fodor, Amsterdam
Scanning 1990, Deweer Art Gallery, Otegem (B) (cat.)
1991
Dutch entry 21a Bienal internacional de São Paulo, Stedelijk Van Abbemuseum, Eindhoven (cat.)
21a Bienal internacional de São Paulo, São Paulo (cat.)
1993
Recto / Verso (Signalen 3), ICA Institute of Contemporay Art, Amsterdam (cat.)
Festival aan de Werf, Utrecht
Peiling 1993, Centraal Museum, Utrecht (cat.)
1994
Ik + de Ander: dignity for all, reflection on humanity, Beurs van Berlage, Amsterdam (cat.)
Spellbound: Inez van Lamsweerde, David Bade, Aernout Mik, Stedelijk Museum Bureau Amsterdam, Amsterdam; Centro Cultural de Bélem, Lissabon; Asociación Cultural Cruce, Madrid (leaflet)
Het Zevende Museum, Stroom Haags Centrum Beeldende Kunst, The Hague (cat.)
1995
A night at the show, Field, Zurich
La valise du célibatair; De koffer van de celibatair, Central Station, Maastricht (leaflet)
Wild Walls, Stedelijk Museum, Amsterdam (cat.)
1996
Gedraag Je!.. / Behave!.., Stedelijk Museum Bureau Amsterdam, Amsterdam (leaflet)
Abendland: Berend Strik, Aernout Mik, Renée Kool, throughout Munster (curated by Städtische Ausstellungshalle Am Hawerkamp and Theater im

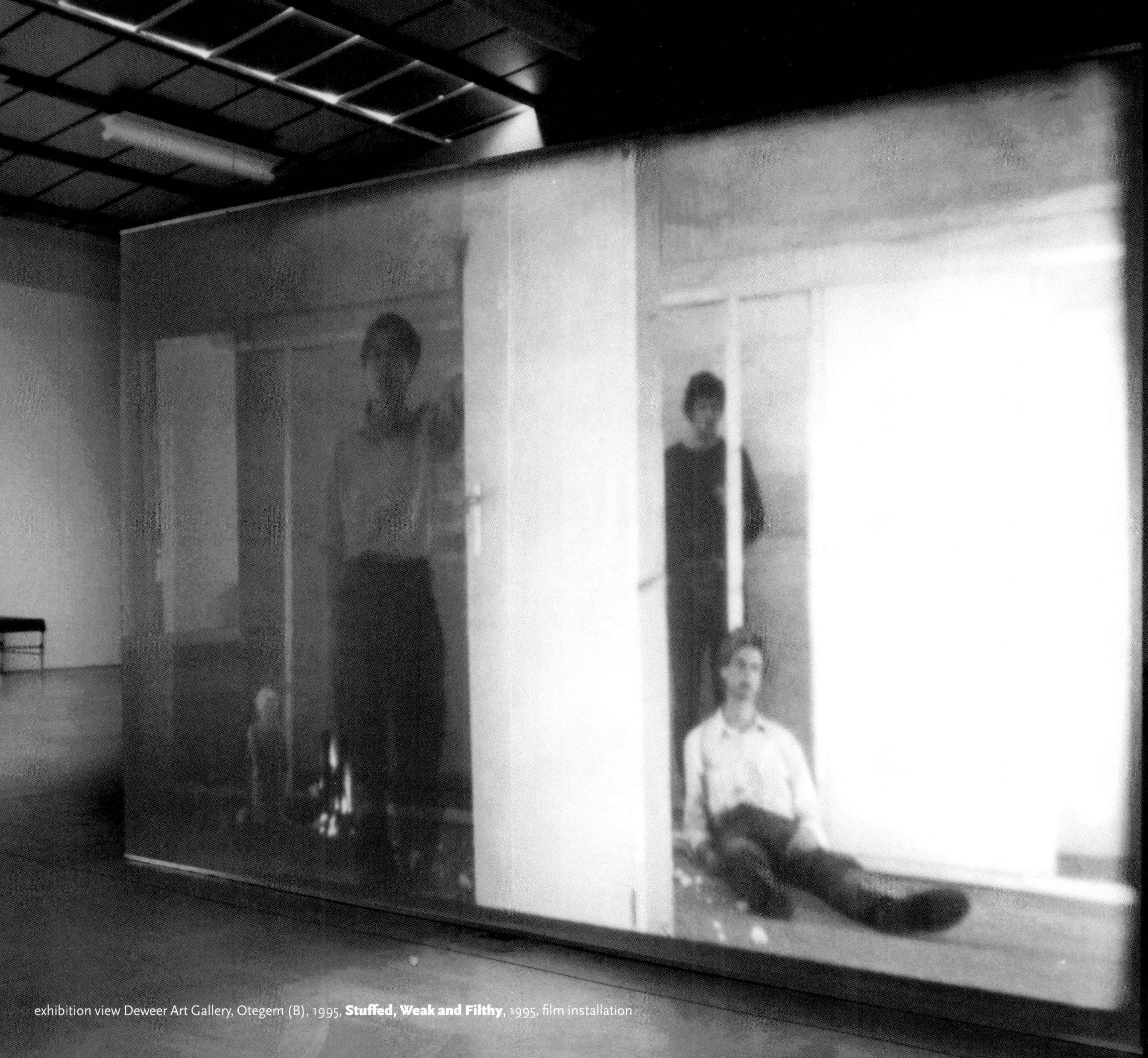

exhibition view Deweer Art Gallery, Otegem (B), 1995, **Stuffed, Weak and Filthy**, 1995, film installation

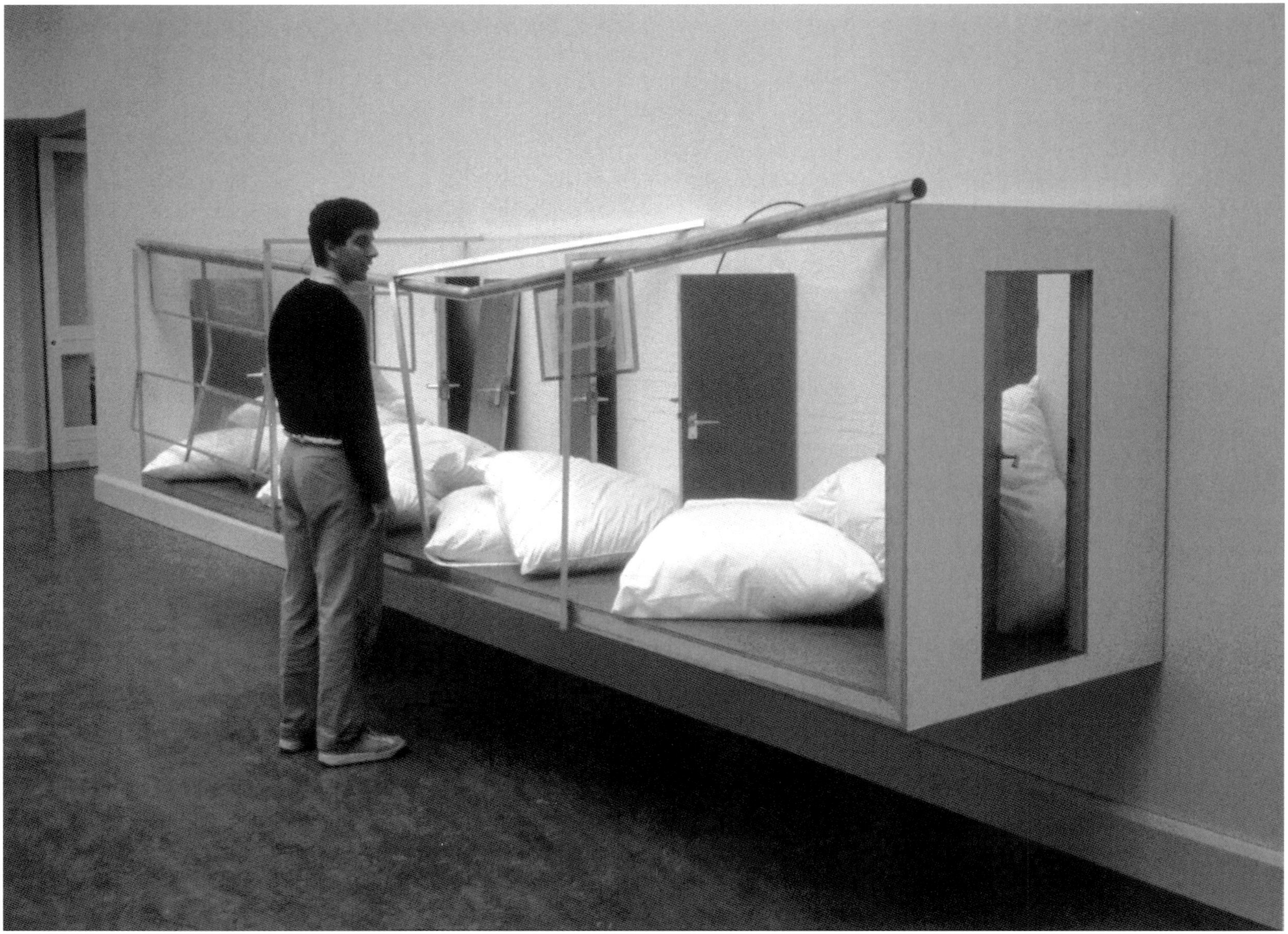

 exhibition view Stedelijk Van Abbemuseum, Eindhoven, 1991, **Miscellaneous Exits for Smaller Animals**, 1991, mixed media sculpture

Pumpenhaus, Munster) (cat.)
Watou '96: Wereld je bent een geduldig woord, throughout Watou (cat.)
The Scream, Arken Museum of Modern Art, Copenhagen (cat.)
ID. An international survey on the notion of identity in contemporary art, Stedelijk Van Abbemuseum, Eindhoven; Le Nouveau Musée, Villeurbanne (cat.)

1997

Booster Up Dutch Courage, L.A. International Biennial, Los Angeles; W139, Amsterdam (cat.)
Screen surface & Narrative Space, Museum of Photography, Helsinki
été 97, Centre genevois de gravure contemporaine, Geneva
Standort Berlin: Places to stay, Büro Friedrich, Berlin
Personal Absurdities, Galerie Gebauer, Berlin

1998

Do All Oceans Have Walls?, Gesellschaft für Aktuelle Kunst, Bremen (cat.)
Ironisch / Ironic, Museum für Gegenwartskunst, Zurich (with Marjoleine Boonstra) (cat.)
Triple X Festival, Westergasfabriek, Amsterdam (leaflet)
Grown in Frozen Time, Shed im Eisenwerk, Frauenfeld
Déplacements, Rue du Cherche-Midi / Galerie Anton Weller, Paris
Roommates, Museum van Loon, Amsterdam (cat.)
Mise en Scène, Grazer Kunstverein, Graz (cat.)
Pictures for the Blue Room, NIFCA. The Nordic Institute of Contemporary Art, Helsinki; Vigeland Museum, Oslo (cat.)

1999

A Touch of... Evil, Metrònom Fundació Rafael Tous d'Art Contemporani, Barcelona
Nur Wasser lässt sich leichter schneiden, Hedrichsmühle, Neumühlen-Hamburg
Hollandkindergartenjapanbondage, De Vleeshal, Middelburg
Tales of the Tip: Art on Garbage, former rubbish-dump, Bavel-Breda (curated by Stichting Fundament, Breda and Praktijkburo, Amsterdam) (cat.)
EXTRAetORDINAIRE, Printemps de Cahors, Cahors (cat.)
Panorama 2000: Art in Utrecht seen from the Dom Tower, throughout Utrecht (curated by Centraal Museum, Utrecht) (cat.)
Signs of Life, Melbourne Biennial, Melbourne (cat.)
Glad ijs, Stedelijk Museum, Amsterdam
Ex-tension, Museum Het Domein, Sittard (CD-Rom)
Hanging Around, Projektraum Museum Ludwig, Cologne (cat.)
Post.tragi.KoMik, Palazzo dell' Papese, Centro Arte Contemporanea, Siena (cat.)
In All the Wrong Places, Ottawa Art Gallery, Ottawa
Spread, Galleri Index, Stockholm

Bibliography

Texts by the artist (a selection)

1993

'Sandwiches', *Metropolis M*, Vol. 14, No. 2 (April), p. 6
'Over een kleine trap', *Archis*, No. 10 (October), p. 11

1995

'Blauwe gum; Blue Gum', *Kunst & Museumjournaal*, Vol. 6, No. 5, p. 51

1996

'Toilet maken', *Liza May Post*, Artimo Foundation, Breda, pp. 6-9

Catalogues, articles and reviews (a selection)

1992

C. van Winkel, 'A gentle collapsing. Over de attributen van Aernout Mik', *Metropolis M*, Vol. 13, No. 1 (February), pp. 28-31
M. Kremer, 'Entertainment of het breekbare geloof in een medium', *Kunst & Museumjournaal*, Vol. 4, No. 2, pp. 49-53
J. Coucke, 'Aernout Mik. Für Nichts und Wieder Nichts', exh.cat. *Aernout Mik*, Deweer Art Gallery, Otegem (B), w.p.

1993

M. Kremer, 'Barbarella of pleidooi voor de permanente onevenwichtigheid', *Kunst & Museumjournaal*, Vol. 4, No. 6, pp. 57-61
M. Kremer, 'De wedergeboorte van het drama', *Kunst & Museumjournaal*, Vol. 5, No. 2, pp. 51-52
P. Gijsberts, 'Aernout Mik en Adam Kalkin', *Metropolis M*, Vol. 14, No. 1 (February), p. 50
C. van Winkel, 'Aernout Mik en Adam Kalkin: "The Philosophy of Furniture"', *Archis*, No. 3 (March), pp. 12-13
F. Hettig, 'Adam Kalkin-Aernout Mik: '"The Philosophy of Furniture"', *Forum International*, Vol. IV, No. 17 (March-April), p. 125
A. Marx, 'Uitdagend en ontregelend. Woningen en politiebureau van Ton Venhoeven in Amsterdam', *De Architekt*, No. 10, pp. 100-105

1994
M. Kremer, C. van Winkel, 'The word art, you know, is not my primary interest. Interview with Aernout Mik', *Archis*, No. 1 (January), pp. 68-74
D. Ruyters, 'Peiling '93', *Metropolis M*, Vol. 15, No. 1 (February), pp. 46-47
P. Gijsberts, 'Close encounter: 45 Seniorenwoningen en 1 politiebureau van Ton Venhoeven', *Archis*, No. 5 (May), pp. 36-41
1995
M. Kremer, 'The life of a Repo Man is always intense. Richard Hoeck, Aernout Mik, Joëlle Tuerlinckx: scenario's voor een hernieuwde inbezitneming van de institutionele kunstruimte', *Archis*, No. 6 (June), pp. 70-80
E. Karcher, 'Aernout Mik', *Art. Das Kunstmagazin*, No. 10 (October), p. 72
L. ter Braak, 'Aernout Mik', *Metropolis M*, Vol. 16, No. 6 (December), p. 47
L. Coelewij, M. van Nieuwenhuyzen, 'Wild Walls', exh.cat. *Wild Walls*, Stedelijk Museum, Amsterdam, pp. 47-92
J. Coucke, 'Aernout Mik', exh.cat. *Aernout Mik*, Deweer Art Gallery, Otegem (B), w.p.
1996
S. van der Meulen, 'De wonderlijke wereld van Aernout Mik', *De Kunsten, tijdschrift van de Hogeschool voor de Kunsten Arnhem*, Vol. 5, No. 1 (March), pp. 29-32
R. Kersting, 'Aernout Mik: Langer oder liegender Affe Servatiiplatz Münster', exh.cat. *Abendland: Berend Strik, Aernout Mik, Renée Kool*, Städtische Ausstellungshalle Am Hawerkamp, Munster, pp. 2-4
1997
M. Lind, 'Stillsam och lyrisk Holländsk surrealism', *Svenska Dagblad*, August 2
M. Kremer, 'Über Aernout Mik. Ein heiterer Nihilist trinkt Orangensaft und isst dazu ein Brownie', *Artist Kunstmagazin*, Heft 27, No. 2 (November), pp. 26-29 Published in English exh.cat. *ID. An international survey on the notion of identity in contemporary art*, Stedelijk Van Abbemuseum, Eindhoven, pp. 63-65
C. van Winkel, 'Excursion with Tennis Balls, Shiny Knees and Green Slime', exh.cat. *Aernout Mik, Willem Oorebeek*, XLVII Biennale di Venezia: Padiglione Olandese, Venice, pp. 59-105
M. Kopsa, 'The problem (un)solved', exh.cat. *Dutch Courage*, L.A. International Biennial, Los Angeles; W139, Amsterdam, pp. 24-25
1998
W. Sütö, 'Schemergebied vol slapstick en horror', *de Volkskrant*, July 3
S.N., 'Aernout Mik', *BT9, Monthly Art Magazine Bijutsu Techno*, Vol. 50, No. 761 (September), pp. 64-65, 82
L. ter Braak, 'Willem Oorebeek & Aernout Mik: Reinventing realities', *Flash Art*, Vol. XXXI, No. 203 (November-December), pp. 94-95
J. Guldemond, 'Aernout Mik. Wie die Räume gefüllt werden müssen', exh.cat. *NL. Hedendaagse kunst uit Nederland rondom de collectie van het Van Abbemuseum*, Stedelijk Van Abbemuseum, Eindhoven, pp. 76-81
H. Griese, 'Aernout Mik', exh.cat. *Do All Oceans Have Walls?*, Museum für Aktuelle Kunst, Bremen, pp. 90-91
J. Guldemond, 'Hongkongoria', exh.cat. *Ironisch / Ironic*, Museum für Gegenwartskunst, Zurich, pp. 187-192
J. van Adrichem, 'Aernout Mik', exh.cat. *René Magritte en de hedendaagse kunst / René Magritte and contemporary art*, PMMK. Museum voor Moderne Kunst, Oostende, pp. 158-161
1999
M. van Nieuwenhuyzen, 'Hanging around', exh. cat. *Rotation, Part I: Hanging Around*, Museum Ludwig, Cologne
J. Engberg, 'Aernout Mik', exh. cat. *Signs of Life*, Melbourne Biennial, Melbourne

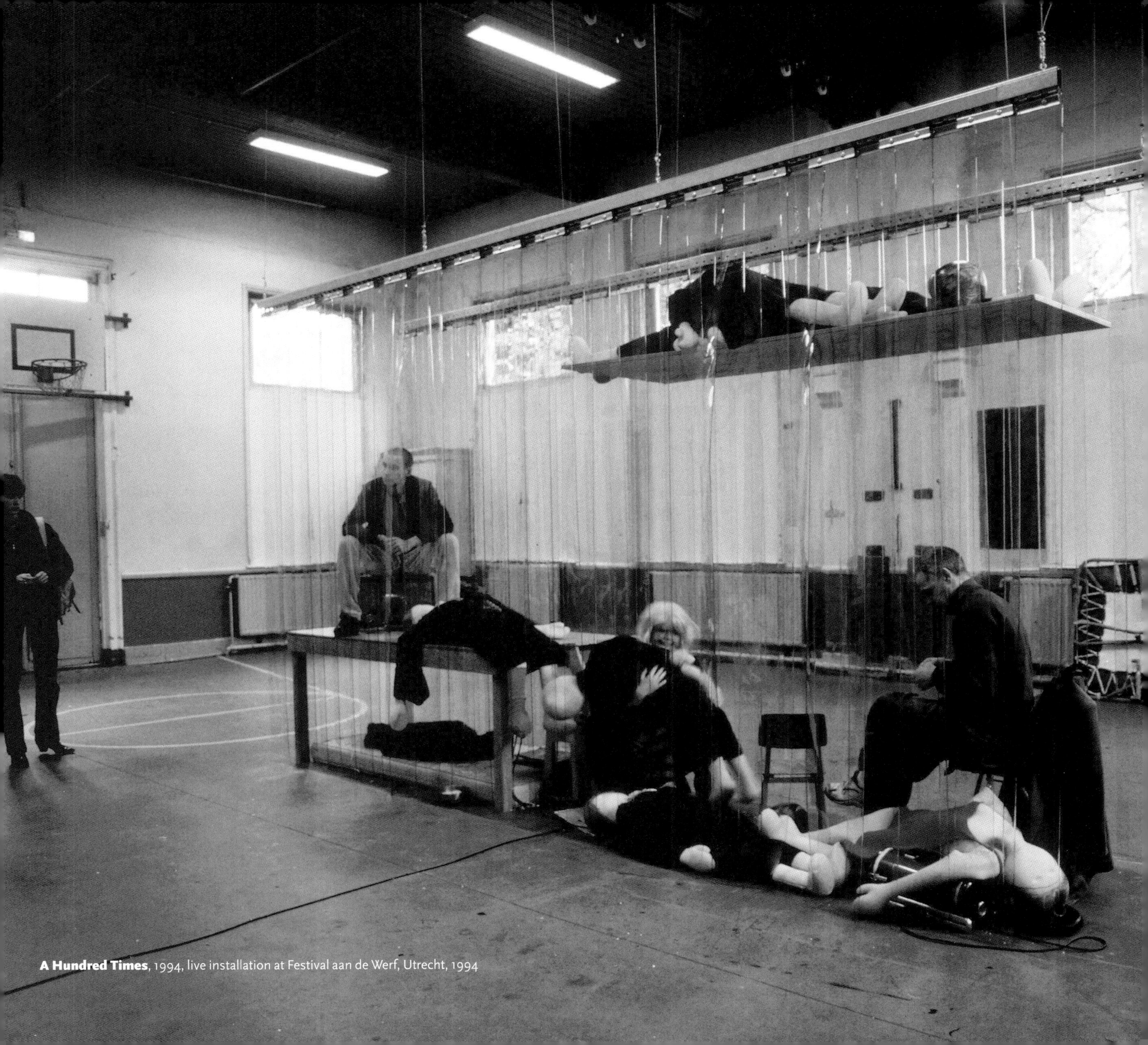

A Hundred Times, 1994, live installation at Festival aan de Werf, Utrecht, 1994

Colophon

Aernout Mik, primal gestures, minor roles appears on the occasion of the exhibition of the same name in the Stedelijk Van Abbemuseum, Eindhoven, 29 January – 27 March 2000

Stedelijk Van Abbemuseum

DIRECTOR
Jan Debbaut
DEPUTY DIRECTOR
Frank Lubbers

Exhibition

CURATOR
Jaap Guldemond
EXHIBITIONS MANAGER
Marijke Roef
SECRETARY
Golda Maas
REGISTRAR
Bert de Graaf
INSTALLATION
The technical staff of the Van Abbemuseum under supervision of Theo Wajon
ACKNOWLEDGEMENTS
the artist and the lenders to the exhibition
THE ARTIST WISHES TO THANK
Bart Aptroot, Demcon BV Hengelo, Norah Grace, Jaap Hoogerdijk, Adam Kalkin, Rob Nissink, Joke Treffers (de Beeldverwerkers) Amsterdam, Jos Willem van Oorschot, Singel Film, Venhoeven c.s., all the actors, etc.
VIDEO WORKS
Camera, directing and editing assistant: Marjoleine Boonstra
Lighting: Benito Strangio
Production assistants: Xander Karskens, Maxine Kopsa
Technical assistant: Marc Claeijs
Special effects: Rob's Prop shop (*Softer Catwalk in Collapsing Rooms, Swab, Portrait*), Amsterdam
Video colour correction: Ronald van Dieren, Hans Buiting NOB, Hilversum

Several of Mik's works were sponsored by The Netherlands Foundation for Fine Arts, Design and Architecture, Amsterdam, and the Mondrian Foundation, Amsterdam. This publication was financially supported by the Mondrian Foundation, Amsterdam.

Publication

EDITING
Jaap Guldemond, Aernout Mik
DESIGN
Arlette Brouwers, Amsterdam/Emst
in cooperation with Aernout Mik, Amsterdam
BIOGRAPHY-BIBLIOGRAPHY
Diana Franssen
COPY EDITING
Astrid Vorstermans, NAi Publishers
Paula Vaandrager, Amsterdam
PRODUCTION
Astrid Vorstermans, NAi Publishers
TRANSLATIONS
Texts Tijs Goldschmidt, Jaap Guldemond, Mark Kremer (D-E): Peter Mason, Amsterdam
Text Bernhard Balkenhol (G-E): Michael Stoeber and Audrey Mei, Hanover
PUBLISHER
Stedelijk Van Abbemuseum, Eindhoven
NAi Publishers, Rotterdam
PHOTOGRAPHY
Christian Augustin, Pieter Boersma, Marjoleine Boonstra, Bernd Borchardt, Peter Cox, Jannes Linders, Lydia van Marissing, Mikkel McAlinden, Frank Pusch & Helmut Wieben, Gerald van Rafelghem,Gert Jan van Rooij, Tomasz Samek, Lothar Schrempf, Ewald Timmermans, Tim Wickens
DIGITAL PROCESSING OF VIDEO STILLS
Martinus Meiborg, Broadware, Amsterdam
PRINTING & LITHOGRAPHY
Lecturis bv, Eindhoven
TYPEFACE
FFScala Sans

The Stedelijk Van Abbemuseum and NAi Publishers will simultaneously publish a Dutch edition of this publication: ISBN 90-70149-75-3

Available in North, South and Central America through D.A.P./ Distributed Art Publishers Inc, 155 Sixth Avenue 2nd Floor, New York, NY 10013-1507, Tel. 212 627.1999, Fax 212 627.9484

Available in the U.K. and Ireland through Art Data, 12 Bell Industrial Estate 50 Cunnington Street, London W4 5HB, Tel. 181 747.1061, Fax 181 742.2319

Printed and Bound in the Netherlands

English edition: ISBN 90-70149-77-X

COVER
still from video installation **Softer Catwalk in Collapsing Rooms**, 1999